Alternatives to Violence

David A. Wolfe
Christine Wekerle
Katreena Scott

"Alternatives to Violence"

Empowering
Youth to
Develop
Healthy
Relationships

SAGE Publications
International Educational and Professional Publisher
Thousand Oaks   London   New Delhi

For information address:

SAGE Publications, Inc.
2455 Teller Road
Thousand Oaks, California 91320
E-mail: order@sagepub.com

SAGE Publications Ltd.
6 Bonhill Street
London EC2A 4PU
United Kingdom

SAGE Publications India Pvt. Ltd.
M-32 Market
Greater Kailash I
New Delhi 110048 India

Printed in the United States of America

Library of Congress Cataloging-in-Publication Data

Wolfe, David A.
    Alternatives to violence: Empowering youth to develop healthy
relationships / David A. Wolfe, Christine Wekerle, Katreena Scott.
      p. cm.
    Includes bibliographical references and index.
    ISBN 0-8039-7030-7 (alk. paper).—ISBN 0-8039-7031-5 (pbk.:
alk. paper)
      1. Family violence—Canada—Prevention. 2. Dating violence—
Canada—Prevention. 3. Interpersonal relations in adolescence—
Study and teaching—Canada. 4. Social work with youth—Canada.
5. Youth Relationships Project (London, Ont.) I. Werkerle,
Christine. II. Scott, Katreena. III. Title.
HV6626.23.C2W65   1996
362.82′927′0971—dc20
                                        96-25384

97 98 99 00 01 02 10 9 8 7 6 5 4 3 2

Acquiring Editor:	C. Terry Hendrix
Editorial Assistant:	Dale Grenfell
Production Editor:	Sanford Robinson
Production Assistant:	Sherrise Purdum
Typesetter/Designer:	Danielle Dillahunt
Cover Designer:	Lesa Valdez
Print Buyer:	Anna Chin

To our families:
Barb, Alex, Amy, and Anne (DW)
Mike, Celeste, Christian, Colin, and Carson (CW)
Cherry, Jerry, Garth, and Helen (KS)

Contents

Preface

This book was inspired by the fundamental belief that current policies aimed at addressing personal violence (i.e., woman abuse, rape, child physical and sexual abuse) are obsolete, ineffective, and deceptive to the public. Personal violence has always been a major (although carefully hidden) epidemic that appears to be self-generating across generations, yet society has tragically failed to respond in kind. Rather than looking for ways to *control* violence, however, we have chosen in this book and in our related manual (*The Youth Relationships Manual*; Wolfe et al., 1996) to develop practical ways to *promote healthy, nonviolent relationships*. We are guided as well by the belief that, in the long run, prevention is cheaper, more effective, and more humane than the vast majority of our current efforts at detection, deterrence, punishment, or containment.

We contend that the existing knowledge base of personal violence is sufficient to mount more meaningful efforts to curtail the perpetuation of these patterns. Relationships, especially those formed in childhood and adolescence, with caregivers, peers, and intimate partners, are both the training ground and the mode of expression of much personal violence. Consequently, we feel that determinants of healthy relationships suggest new pathways to follow in the prevention of intimate violence. Youth, by virtue of their developmental level, motivation, current interests, and future needs, are well suited for the investment of this time and energy.

Because personal violence affects everyone to some extent, we cannot just isolate known offenders; rather, the time has arrived to reexamine our social institutions and cultural values that perpetuate abuse. We believe it is time for a change in social policy away from expensive and ineffective treatments and punitive sanctions after-the-fact, and more toward a proactive policy that is child, youth, and family centered. Education and skills are needed to facilitate the promotion of healthy, nonviolent relationships, peer support, and social action aimed at ending violence in relationships, to build strengths and resiliency rather than to detect and isolate offenders alone.

For instance, is it worthwhile to view acts of violence as symptoms or indicia of more endemic social issues, rather than a specific disorder of the individual, family, or neighborhood? Can we expect to curtail the growth of violence in society by increasing efforts at detection, law enforcement, and punishment, especially of the more public (but by far less common) forms of violence? Have prevention efforts aimed at health-related problems (e.g., AIDS, drug abuse, smoking, and so on) taught us anything that could be of value in preventing violence in relationships, especially among youth?

To address these possibilities we have developed this book in relation to several themes, which set the stage for a health promotion effort aimed at building healthy, nonviolent relationships among youth:

1. *The expression of violence is most commonly seen in the context of relationships.*

Based on principles of youth participation and value, we promote throughout this book the importance of developing relationships based on equality and balance. By defining violence as an issue of power over another, rather than physical injury alone, the relationship itself becomes an important area of concern. This viewpoint contradicts our deepest beliefs in what defines violent acts and violent persons, largely due to a strong societal focus on the most visible and disconcerting forms of violence.

The media provides daily messages of the most newsworthy acts of violence, often between strangers or against groups, which may leave us with the impression that such actions are due to a disturbed individual who is different from the rest of us. Due to the considerable effort, however, that has been directed toward discovering the root causes of violence, we now recognize that despite these news portrayals and stereotyped images of violent offenders, violent acts are not limited predominantly to attacks by strangers.

2. *Current policies to address personal violence are outdated and superficial.*

Imagine attempting to cure AIDS by focusing only on the most serious cases. We have long recognized that such an approach would be expensive and largely unproductive in the long-term—instead, public health officials have deemed it necessary to look beyond the symptoms to the causes and the major influences of AIDS-related disorders, to prevent the disease before it happens. The prevention of violence involves many of the same tactics: We cannot expect to make a significant dent in the incidence of violent and abusive acts, without considering at least the co-occurrence of alternative messages, models, and principles for developing healthy, nonviolent relationships.

Despite the obvious lack of success of current policies toward violence, we find it telling that such policies continue to focus on the most visible and personally frightening forms of violence—street and school violence, predominantly among *youth*—and too often ignore the more systemic and pathognomic forms of violence in the home that establish the pathways to the next generation. In contrast, a health promotion paradigm becomes the foundation for the issues and solutions raised throughout this book, both in terms of understanding the nature of violence in relationships as well as offering the most fruitful solutions.

3. *Violence does not affect everyone equally—it is ingrained in cultural expressions of power and inequality, and affects women, children, and minorities most significantly.*

As noted throughout this book, women's longstanding inequality has a powerful impact on their life experiences, and especially their male-female relationships. To be effective as a prevention program, efforts must reflect the reality of women's lives—the inequality and relative imbalance of power, as well as the nature of adolescent relationships in general.

> 4. *Prevention of violence entails building on the positive (through empowerment) in the context of relationships, not just focusing on individual weaknesses or deviance.*

Empowerment plays a very important role in redressing the inequalities and imbalances that contribute to the abuse of power. Empowerment refers to the motivation, freedom, and capacity to direct one's life purposefully and in harmony with others (Surrey, 1991). Amaro (1995) adds to this definition the notion of power through *connection,* which differs from the traditional meaning of power that is associated with having more control or power over others. Helping youth to connect with one another and to share their common experiences and concerns generates both personal power and important resources for change.

> 5. *Youth are important resources and are part of the solution.*

An important consideration for change is timing. In this regard, theory and research highlight the formative intimate relationship years of adolescence as a critical point in the development of violent relationships or for changing the trend toward violence. Adolescence marks the stage where primary affective ties are being moved from the family to the peer network and romantic partnerships. As a consequence, adolescence is a "window" of opportunity to change historically reinforced proviolence relationship themes, such as male entitlement, dominance, and aggression, and female passivity and deference. These relationship themes emerge again and again across the various forms of interpersonal violence—child abuse, domestic violence, date rape—urging researchers to uncover common roots and to isolate developmental pathways of violence.

Turning the Corner:
The Importance of Participatory
Education and Empowerment

Drawing from recent studies concerned with the formation of healthy relationships, this book will explore how healthy relationships can be formed in a manner that reduces the overall risk to women of being abused or mistreated by their partners, as well as the risk to men of becoming abusive. Thus, the importance of gender dynamics in the development of healthy versus violent relationships is underscored.

There have been numerous studies and approaches focusing on understanding how people change their behaviors and beliefs, especially related to issues affecting their intimate relationships. We offer our model of how violent relationships may develop, especially during adolescence, and highlight many of the risk factors leading up to such relationship violence. We then present the major tenets and methods that follow from our prevention model, which has become the Youth Relationships Project (YRP).

Helping youth to understand the abuse of power and control in their own relationships, with the goal being to promote more egalitarian relationships, is a workable solution. With our greater understanding of the roots of violence it becomes easier to recognize that "fighting violence" means not only stopping something unwanted from occurring—it also means providing adequate resources and increasing our commitment to youth and families.

The ideas expressed in this book and its companion manual (*The Youth Relationships Manual: A Group Approach to the Prevention of Woman Abuse and the Promotion of Healthy Relationships*) were developed with the thoughtful assistance and interest of many students and colleagues over the past several years, to whom we are most grateful. Robert Gough, Deborah Reitzel-Jaffe, and Carolyn Grasley merit special recognition for their energetic commitment to the development of ideas and activities that are of interest to youth, and for their countless hours facilitating groups with adolescents for the purpose of helping and learning. We have seldom had the pleasure of working with such dedicated individuals, who bring creativity and hope to the prevention of woman and child abuse.

Anna-Lee Pittman, who joined the Youth Relationships Project in 1994 as project manager, deserves our sincere appreciation for her central role in bringing the project to life and uncomplainingly chasing down every article, every research site, and every funding possibility that we managed to identify. Her assistance to other members of the project and her devotion to the community, to youth, and to ending violence against women and children have gained the respect of us all. We also sincerely thank Jennifer Stumpf, Andrea McEachern, and Lorrie Lefebvre for their ideas and hard work in developing the research tools so desperately needed to advance this field.

The authors are also indebted to the teachers and administration of the London Board of Education and the London/Middlesex County Board of Education for their stalwart efforts to introduce this program into several of their schools. We thank the many committed individuals from Children's Aid Societies across southwestern Ontario who have helped in many untold ways to organize and conduct the Youth Relationships Program with young people receiving assistance from their agencies.

Finally, we express our appreciation to the federal and provincial funding agencies and foundations that were instrumental both in providing an opportunity to try out our ideas (with very little to go on at the time) and in establishing the research and service plan that became the YRP. We acknowledge (in alphabetical order) the support of Health Canada (Family Violence Prevention Division and the National Health Research and Development Program), the Institute for the Prevention of Child Abuse (Province of Ontario), and the Ontario Mental Health Foundation (Province of Ontario). Although we accept full responsibility for the ideas expressed herein, we are grateful for the helpful feedback and assistance received from each of these funding agencies over the course of developing and testing our research and intervention ideas.

DAVID A. WOLFE
CHRISTINE WEKERLE
KATREENA SCOTT

CHAPTER ONE

A Call for Action

Violence in the Lives of
Children, Youth, and Families

For Immediate Release:
Social Disease Identified as *Odium*

Imagine that when you open up today's paper you are greeted by the following information concerning an as-yet unexplained disease, which scientists have tentatively labeled *Odium*. You scan the article with interest to learn what is known about Odium. See Box 1.1.

The article concludes on a bit of a frightening note: These informed scientists are pessimistic about discovering any biological, psychological, practical, or ethical way to isolate persons at risk of spreading Odium before they harm others—*everyone, to some extent, has been infected!* Thus, they favor looking into a broad public health strategy to address the known and suspected underlying causes of Odium that affect every person to a greater or lesser extent.

1

BOX 1.1
Odium Worries Scientists

Scientists at the Center for Social Disease Control today released the most recent figures on the newest social disease to plague North America—Odium. Speaking conservatively, Dr. Annette Harper estimated that the disease may affect somewhere between 10% to 40% of the North American population during their lifetime, and may induce death and permanent injury in children as well as adults.

Dr. Harper confirmed previous reports that scientists believe that the harmful impact of Odium affects women and children most directly, and that cultural, racial, ethnic, and other visible minorities are in greatest jeopardy of being harmed by the disease. Recent findings indicate that Odium is spread in many ways—through contact with other Odious individuals, through ignorance, through the abuse of power—and that males are at greatest risk of being "silent carriers" from early adolescence through adulthood.

Persons who test positive for Odium are said to deny that it is a problem for them, or that they have it, or that it even exists, which has amazed both researchers and the public alike.

Scientists explained that they have been unsuccessful in alerting the general population to this problem; it's considered by laypersons to be a private problem. They are told, after all, that "individuals who complain about odious persons *should have known better* than to hang out in odious-infected areas, or to behave or dress in an odious-attracting manner."

The professional community has shared their knowledge on the background of persons who have Odium, discovering that such individuals share in common very significant developmental and familial experiences that are *negative*, and they generally lack healthy relationships, social supports, and similar *positive* experiences enjoyed by nonodious individuals.

Researchers and clinicians have come a long way in understanding what motivates someone with Odium to dominate women (for example), what he thinks and believes about the use of force or manipulation of others, and how he uses emotional or sexual arousal to excuse his decision to behave in an odious manner.

BOX 1.1

Continued

Scientists explained that although many critical questions remain, they have largely eliminated several factors from their list of suspected causes of Odium. They have discovered that Odium respects no boundaries of culture, race, income, or occupational status; however, "those with greater social power and privilege need to be immunized," explained one scientist.

In looking for simple causes, scientists have generally concluded that Odium cannot be explained on the basis of any particular blight alone, such as drugs or alcohol, violent movies or television, violent neighborhoods, or even rock videos. As suspected, they have confirmed that persons who have Odium are not well-adjusted or healthy individuals, although no medical, psychological, or social category fully explains the disease. Moreover, persons who come into contact with them are often scarred in both visible and invisible ways, to which they have been fighting to draw attention.

Knowing these things about Odium, a special panel of government officials and experts has quickly assembled to announce the following frontal attack on the problem. The panel makes the following announcement:

BOX 1.2

Planned Government Action Against Odium

- Efforts to identify and diagnose such persons as "Odious" will be stepped up immediately, so that everyone will know who they are (and the rest of us can be assured that we are not among them). Frightening posters of odious-looking persons are placed in subways, buses, and on television.
- Odium is to be more carefully and narrowly defined, so that only the *most Odious* persons are identified and offered treatment. The cost savings by tightening the criteria is estimated to be enormous!

BOX 1.2
Continued

- Justice officials, coordinating with health, agree to invest millions more to build prisons and special housing facilities, and to hire more police and pass more restrictive laws to control the Odious; this commitment is proclaimed as "the only real solution."
- Child welfare authorities are notified that their mandate and resources are being expanded, expressly for the purpose of investigating child casualties of the odious and to heighten the appearance of safety and concern.
- The attorney general's office vows to "spend whatever it takes" to prove a person is or is not odious, and thus prevent the spread of odium to others and to ensure justice.
- Social services, aware of the growing number of women forced out of their homes and communities by their odious partners, announce plans to build shelters in every corner of every community.
- The Ministry of Education announces a "Zero Tolerance of Odium" policy, and vows to remove any individual from the school system who exhibits symptoms of the disease.

The newspaper reporter, interested in every angle of this breaking news, locates one or two purported cases of odium that do not fit what scientists describe. In a boxed corner of the article, the reporter describes the mandate of the False Odium Foundation and the plight of a local resident who lost his job, his wife and family, and his savings because over-zealous health officials falsely diagnosed him—he explains he was doing his honest best as a father and husband to "teach good values, discipline, and respect" and he was merely exercising his right to do so with his family.

Questioning Our Views
of Violence and Abuse

The previous scenario raises a number of questions and issues that set the stage for a critical discussion of violence in the lives of children, youth, and families. Almost every day we read in the newspaper about a new episode of violence, often committed by a young adult against another young adult, or an "estranged husband" against his wife and children. The public's growing concern about what is perceived to be a sinister, uncontrollable tide of crime feeds both a sense of fear as well as efforts at self-protection, stricter laws, and longer jail sentences. Elected officials, attempting to shift priorities in favor of safety and protection for citizens, argue that society has been too lax and too lenient for too long—we need to get tough on crime to reclaim our streets.

Understandably, we are caught in the middle of a dilemma in which we are angered by the level of violence, frustrated by the perceived ineffectiveness of the courts, and increasingly unsympathetic to the underlying social causes.

Yet, as we consider the seriousness and complexity of the issues involved and strive to find ready solutions for controlling violence, we must also ponder why North American culture has become increasingly more violent over the past several decades. Although we may admit there is more to it, many of us are still inclined to attribute violence to characterological factors found especially among identifiable persons, groups, or races (Swim, Aikin, Hall, & Hunter, 1995). This aggregated perspective (that is, all of the suspected reasons for violent behavior can be accounted for in the nature of these individuals or groups) allows us to maintain caution while in public, and to project most (if not all) of the blame for violence and crime onto these identifiable targets (LaGrange & Ferraro, 1989). These targets are familiar to us all—persons of color and persons of foreign origin; women and homosexuals; persons who lack education, live in bad neighborhoods, or whom we generically refer to as "youth."

Whereas the problem of violence in our communities remains extremely troubling, it may represent only the visible aspects of a less pronounced but more widespread phenomenon: personal relationships, ranging from parent/child to husband/wife, too often are marred by physical and emotional abuse. Although as yet unproven, the notion that "violence breeds violence" remains viable and probable (Widom, 1989). After more than 30 years of study and description, it is still a more likely perception to view street crime and youth violence, in particular, as the most serious, escalating, and dangerous problems in our communities, and fail to grasp the scope or seriousness of violence in the lives of women, children, and youth in our families. As Senator Joseph Biden, Jr. (Delaware) recently stated:

> If the leading newspapers were to announce tomorrow a new disease that, over the past year, had afflicted from 3 to 4 million citizens, few would fail to appreciate the seriousness of the illness. Yet, when it comes to the 3 to 4 million women who are victimized by violence each year, the alarms ring softly. We live in a nation that has 3 times as many animal shelters as battered women's shelters. We live in a nation where crimes against women are still perceived as anything but a crime—as a family problem, as a private matter, as "sexual miscommunication." (Biden, 1993, p. 1059)

A statement by the U.S. Advisory Board on Child Abuse and Neglect (1990) echoes Senator Biden's despair: "It remains, more than 30 years after the announcement of the 'battered child syndrome,' easier to phone someone and report your neighbor for abusing a family member than it does to phone or ask for any type of service to prevent such acts" (p. 3).

Research findings gathered over the past decade underscore the pervasiveness of "intimate violence" (Gelles & Straus, 1988), which is sometimes misconstrued as being less serious than other forms of violence by the mere fact that it is so commonplace. For example, approximately 28% of Canadian women are battered by their partners at some time during their relationship (Statistics Canada, 1993), and in the United States physical abuse is the leading cause of injuries to women between the ages of 15 to 44 years—more common than auto accidents, muggings, and cancer deaths combined (U.S. Senate Judiciary Committee, 1992). Child physical abuse, moreover, is a leading cause of injuries to children and youth and a leading cause of death among infants and toddlers in the United States (U.S. Advisory Board on Child Abuse and Neglect, 1995).

Sexual assault occurs, on average, every 6 minutes in North America (DiCamio, 1993), and many of these victims are under the age of 18 years. We need to be more concerned by the fact that over one quarter (27%) of women are sexually assaulted in their lifetime, usually by someone they know (Rogers, 1994), and that most (60%) college-age men say they would force sexual relations with a woman under the "right" circumstances (Check & Malamuth, 1983).

In their goals for the year 2000, the U.S. Public Health Service specifically targeted adolescents for risk reduction efforts aimed at nutrition, physical activity/fitness, substance use, sexual behavior, violence, accidental injuries, oral and mental health (U.S. Advisory Board on Child Abuse and Neglect, 1991). The rationale for such a plan has become obvious: The three primary causes of mortality during adolescence are injury, homicide, and suicide (Millstein, Petersen, & Nightingale, 1993), which together are responsible for 75% of adolescent deaths. Disturbingly, mortality rates increase by more than 200% between early (ages 10-14) and later (15-19) adolescence, with blacks showing the lowest life expectancy and males dying at a rate more than twice that of females (Millstein et al., 1993).

What issues, if any, are common to women, children, and youth that could inform us about the prevention of violence in relationships? One similarity is that these individuals all share some degree of inequality, due to their gender, age, or related characteristics that may place them in a second-class position. Such inequality is often accompanied by disempowerment and marginalization, factors that lead to feelings of alienation, discrimination, and fear and that become the seeds of both violent behavior and victimization experiences (Amaro, 1995). Thus, if there are common elements behind the vastly different actions we label "violent" or "abusive," they might inform us of ways to formulate common solutions for prevention.

The premise that violence and abuse are neither necessary nor inevitable features of intimate relationships forms the foundation of an alternative strategy. Even among children and youth who have grown up with violence, major shifts in how they relate to others can and do happen (Farber & Egeland, 1987; Herrenkohl, Herrenkohl, & Egolf, 1994). When such shifts from coercive to cooperative behavior do occur (and they are the exception rather than the rule), in many cases the active ingredients involved the prominent influence of healthy, nonviolent individuals (such as teachers, foster parents, grandparents, and so on), the strength and resources of the child or youth (e.g., intelligence, good schools, and other learning opportunities), and an ambient climate of alternative, positive models and resources (Rutter, 1987). In contrast, there is little evidence to support the assumption that "correction" will occur on the basis of out-of-home placement (Shealy, 1995) or punitive sanctions (Doob, Marinos, & Varma, 1995), especially in the absence of any of the above positive influences. This basic premise (i.e, that violence and abuse are neither necessary nor inevitable features of intimate relationships), as yet unproven, leads us to pursue definitions of violence and abuse that are *capable of modification*, and to outline an approach to relationship conflict that is proactive, comprehensive, and health promoting.

Our discussion of alternatives to violence begins with a consideration of the implications of violence, both in terms of powerlessness and alienation as well as the more familiar physical injury and harm. Some of the growing concerns related to school violence, community violence, television violence, and violence in our families and in our relationships are then described, not in an effort to blame or highlight any particular causes or groups of individuals who are more violent than others but rather to look at the common issues inherent across many of these forms of violence. The final section of the chapter returns to a critical examination of how we currently respond to violence, which leads us to plan for more innovative and thoughtful actions.

The Implications of Violence

Violence as Injury and Harm

For the purpose of designing prevention activities, violence and abuse are first defined in relation to a wide range of behaviors, some of which might appear at first to be relatively innocuous, rather than focusing solely on the more recognizable forms. A wide net is cast for the particular purpose of showing the interconnections among verbal and emotional abuse, for example, and the development of more extreme aggression; moreover, prevention activities are not bound by the same restrictions as treatment programs may be, allowing us more freedom to enter into a discussion of abusive behavior without the need to identify or blame particular individuals for their actions. That is, treatment efforts, by definition, are usually restricted to efforts designed to change existing behavior patterns after the fact, which necessitates somewhat strict criteria for defining who "needs" treatment. In contrast, prevention efforts are designed to abort such patterns and promote healthy alternatives, so that the focus of defining the target behaviors is more on understanding the full range of abusive patterns and learning to anticipate and build nonviolent relationships.

Instead of being restricted to legally defined criteria (which often imply that the person has to be "caught"), researchers in the area of child abuse, woman abuse, sexual assault, and similar forms of violence against persons generally define interpersonal violence along an invisible continuum, ranging from mild (and often unreported) acts of coercion, to extreme and life threatening assaults. We prefer this approach to defining violent/abusive acts, because there is a wide degree of variability in what adults and young adults may consider to be "violent" or inappropriate.

Therefore, despite differences in degree and expression, we emphasize that *violence is any attempt to control or dominate another person* (Wolfe et al., 1996). Accordingly, we emphasize with youth the significance of *nonphysical* expressions of violence, such as isolating one's self or partner; limiting self and partner's gender roles, frequent name calling, controlling/dominating of partner, threats to harm self or partner, intimidation and jealousy; as well as physical (e.g., hitting, punching, pushing, kicking, shoving) and sexual abuse (e.g., nonconsensual sex, unwanted touching, sexual accusations against another person).

Violence as Powerlessness and Inequality

Intimate relationships, by their very nature, expose a person's vulnerabilities and strengths. To achieve closeness, each partner must be willing to self-disclose and share him- or herself openly and with a sense of safety and equality. By being vulnerable, an individual takes a risk and shows a willingness to be seen and heard by his or her partner; by ensuring trust and safety, an individual shows respect for the other person and a willingness to let him or her maintain his or her own individuality and growth.

Disclosing to one's partner represents an investment with risks, and men and women seem to calculate these risks in highly unique ways. For example, interpersonal power seems to be an issue for men when deciding to self-disclose, but not for women. As summarized by Cline (1989): "Women avoid disclosing to elude personal hurt or relational problems while men avoid disclosing to maintain control" (p. 9). The politics of power and intimacy, therefore, play an important role in the formation and maintenance of relationships: Women tend to engage in behaviors that *yield control* whereas men engage in behaviors that function to *establish dominance.* These gender styles are powerful forces that most of us are ill-prepared to understand or resist. Rather than defining a relationship explicitly and communicating clearly, the character of the relationship, what we expect and require, is often defined implicitly at a more abstract level. The early childhood precursors to these patterns are explored in greater depth in Chapter 5.

It is relatively easy to imagine how such gender-based patterns or tendencies, if left unchecked, could become abusive. Each of us may have unstated, deeply ingrained expectations about how the other partner is "supposed" to behave, and these hidden intentions and expectations can emerge in many ways. In particular, when strength and size are combined with a need to establish dominance, the formula for abuse is established; expectations become demands, and demands are met by abusing one's position of strength or power over the other.

Accordingly, the definition of violence also must include the abuse of power and control—the imposition of one's will against another's resistance (Hedley, 1994)—not just physical acts of violence. Thus, abuse of an intimate partner is motivated by control and domination. It is meant to isolate the person, annihilate self-esteem, and psychologically enslave the other individual (Dutton & Golant, 1995).

Power dynamics and gender-based violence are fundamental concepts underlying the different forms of interpersonal violence described below—woman abuse, sexual assault, date rape, child abuse, racism, gay and lesbian bashing, as well as others. To counter the strong messages given to youths from many cultural avenues, they must be provided with informed opportunities to examine the many diverse ways in which the abuse of power is expressed in relationships as well as in the broader society (such as access to resources, jobs, education, protection under the law, representation in government, and so on). In particular, they need to consider ways in which their behavior, and the behavior of others, may be designed to elicit submission and obedience from others (i.e., "controlling"), such as explosive anger, threats to harm others, and attempts to isolate someone from their friends and resources.

The significant role of power in romantic relationships is quite clear. According to a survey of 413 heterosexual dating partners, men are over twice as likely as women to be viewed as having more power (Felmlee, 1994). Imbalances also appear in decision making, emotional involvement, and equity. In general, both men and women in dating relationships believe the male is "getting a better deal." Perhaps due to powerful socialization forces, moreover, this survey found that male dominance (but not equity of power between genders) was associated with greater romantic relationship longevity. Young adults and adolescents may have learned to expect a certain imbalance of power in the relationship—after all, maintaining control is a very powerful socialization force in the background of most boys and men.

Furthermore, violence against women and children breeds on the proliferation of proviolence messages extant in youth culture. Some of the primary misconceptions and myths that are shaped by these cultural messages aimed at youth, and which require them to decipher if they are to develop an immunity, can be described as the following:

- *The status quo works.* Adolescents perceive that those who hold power and show strength are more glorified and more successful, both on a personal level and at a more general societal level. Similarly, women and children, minorities, gay/lesbian, and other nonpower groups are seen by adolescents as holding less power and status, thus paving the way for abuse of power and control (Wolfe, Wekerle, Reitzel-Jaffe, & Gough, 1995).

- *Violence is an acceptable norm in relationships.* Adolescents grow up with violence and abuse of power being modeled all around them, and they fit such behavior into their life experiences constantly. Other than clear physical injuries, violence is seen as "no big deal"; it's part of teasing and play (e.g., girls hit and insult as much or more than boys). The overemphasis on male violence, in particular, is not a good match with adolescents' own day-to-day experiences.

Such cultural messages present a number of obstacles to promoting nonviolence among youth. In the broadest terms, such messages establish and reinforce a fascination with violence. For some, this fascination (coupled with the wide availability of alcohol, drugs, and firearms) offers the necessary springboard to use violence as a means of conflict resolution.

In more specific terms regarding abuse of women and children, youth are faced with a pronounced lack of informed choices and models to disentangle relationship issues infused with sexism, racism, and similar forms of discrimination. As they search for answers to peer and relationship issues they are met by the prevailing expectations and stereotypes of a patriarchal society, gender-based norms and expectations, and socialized aggression that is more often seen being rewarded than being punished. Thus, like modern racism, modern sexism is characterized by the denial of continued discrimination, antagonism toward women's demands, and lack of support for policies designed to assist women (Swim et al., 1995).

Furthermore, young men and women often have difficulty accepting the "gender bias" that they encounter when learning about interpersonal violence—that is, the knowledge that men are perpetrators of serious violence against women, and men's and women's expression of the same behavior cannot be compared as equal. Researchers note that although female partners may be violent, it is only male violence that produces fear in the recipient (Jacobson et al., 1994). Such ability to instill fear is considered to be a primary reason why men can use violence as a means of psychological and social control (it works!). If violence is to be prevented, youth must be encouraged to examine critically the male role in interpersonal violence, and to think about how violence may become a "problem-solving strategy" that has a devastating effect on the relationship. The fact that *not all men commit acts of interpersonal violence* reinforces the "choice" aspect of this behavior.

The Spectrum of Violence

Adolescence is a period of development in which many of the risk factors relating to interpersonal violence, stemming both from childhood and contemporaneous sources, become more pronounced. Yet, adolescence has been virtually ignored in terms of its dynamic importance in establishing a pattern of healthy, nonviolent relationships with intimate partners and future family members. For this reason, we begin our exploration of ways to prevent violence by taking a closer look at violence among and against today's youth, in an effort to redirect our energies toward proactive strategies.

In many of the examples shown throughout this chapter youths are often depicted as the problem, rather than carriers of problems that go far deeper into the cultural and social fabric. This depiction reflects what is generally available to us on a daily basis through the media, where youth violence has become a "hot-topic" (Pryor & McGarrell, 1993). Although they may be sensationalized and isolated examples, the teens who perpetrated or experienced these crimes are real and the consequences and harm are profound. These examples and our discussion of the victims and offenders is presented as an introduction to our premise that violence is a *public health issue*, one that demands more than increasing doses of anticrime medication. Solutions to public health problems more typically require greater awareness, inoculation, and universal participation (Albee, Bond, & Monsey, 1992).

Youths as Perpetrators of Violence

Violence in Schools and Communities

BOX 1.3

In 1992-1993 at the junior-high level in Halifax, Nova Scotia, which has about 3,000 students, there were: 3 fights between students and teachers, 19 threats against teachers, 74 fights among students, 4 knives and 1 handgun seized. In the elementary schools, with more than 7,000 students, there were: 19 fights between teachers and students, 11 threats between students, 108 fights between students, 3 knives seized ("Violence in schools," 1993).

We are all getting used to reading such statistics in our daily newspapers, perhaps almost to the point of habituation and complacency. In Canada, the rate of violent crime climbed 52% between 1981 and 1990 (Statistics Canada, 1993). The United States faces about 23,000 homicides each year, where the lifetime risk of homicide is about 42 per 1,000 for black males and 6 per 1,000 for white males (Roth, 1994). As disconcerting as these figures are, the news is even worse if you are young: Adolescents' exposure to violence is higher in the United States than in any other country in the world—for example, a youth is 15 times more likely than his or her English counterpart to die from homicide (Children's Safety Network, 1991). Again, such risks of death are highest among minority groups, especially African American males between 15-19 years old, and appear to be increasing at an alarming rate—an increase of 111% between the years 1985-1990 (Takanishi, 1993).

Similar statistics are being reported from communities across North America, and concerns about personal safety among youths are rising dramatically. For example, the Central Toronto Youth Services (Ryan, Mathews, & Banner, 1993) surveyed 850 students in Grades 6 to 9 to understand the youths' perceptions of the violence around them, as well as their concerns about their own personal safety, and found that

- half to two thirds of the students felt that there was "some" to "a lot" . of violence in schools;
- 3 out of 10 students felt that they were "sometimes" or "not at all" safe from violence while at school, with females feeling slightly less safe than males;
- 8 out of 10 students reported that they had experienced, or knew someone who had experienced, relatively high-level violent victimization (e.g., assaulted or threatened with a weapon).

Although the students felt that school had become a violent place overall, they also had grown to accept that it is simply a mirror of society's problems related to broken families, increasing gang activity, ethnic and racial conflict, and violence.

Understandably, most of us have little appreciation of how often and what forms of violence actually take place in school and community settings on a regular basis, unless we work in a high school or similar setting. Surveys, however, give us some indication of the "normative violence" that youth experience or commit on a day-to-day basis: About 1 of every 5 high school students reports carrying a firearm, a knife, a razor, club, or other weapon on a regular basis. Approximately 20% of all public school teachers report being verbally abused, 8% report being threatened, and 2% report being physically attacked during the previous year (Riley, 1994).

Youth Violence

> **BOX 1.4**
>
> In Washington, DC, a group of youths robbed, raped, and brutally murdered a middle-aged mother while singing and joking (Zinsmeister, 1990).
>
> In Brooklyn, New York, three teenagers methodically set fire to a homeless couple in 1987. When rubbing alcohol wouldn't ignite the pair, the youths went to a local service station for gasoline, which worked (Zinsmeister, 1990).
>
> In Quebec City, in 1989, two teenage skinheads burst into a man's apartment. For half an hour, they ransacked and vandalized his home, kicked and beat him, shaved his head, ground lighted cigarettes into his chest and shoved sleeping pills down his throat (Came et al., 1989).

Unarguably, the rate of youths charged with violent crimes has increased at a fast rate over the past several years, twice as fast as the rate for adults. In Canada, the average annual increase in youth violence has been 14% since 1986, whereas the rate for adults charged with violent incidents has increased on average 7%. Youth violence in the United States is considered by some to be disproportionately out of control. For example, the rate of homicide among 18- to 24-year-olds increased 62% from 1986 to 1991, and murder among those aged 14-17 has increased 124% (Fox & Pierce, 1994). Although, at times, rates of violence seem to be stabilizing or even decreasing, the experts caution against putting too much faith in single-year "trends." For example, the number of homicides in the United States had fallen by 6% from 1991 to 1992; however, murder rates in 1992 still exceeded those for each of the previous 10 years.

There has also been an apparent reemergence of juvenile gangs in the 1990s as a major crime phenomena, connected to rising poverty and drug use/dealing (Fagan, 1989). A look at the statistics on gangs confirms that there is an increase in violent group behavior: Youth gangs of the 1980s and 1990s are more numerous, more prevalent, and more violent than in the 1950s, probably more so than at any other time in the history of the United States. Record numbers of gang-related incidents are being reported in Los Angeles (where 30% of total homicides were gang connected in 1990; Pinderhughes, 1993), and in Chicago (11%; Pinderhughes, 1993). The problem of youth gangs, historically an American problem, has now become a serious concern in Canada as well, although their prevalence is not firmly established (Came et al., 1989).

Behind the statistics reflecting this rise of youth crime is an even more disconcerting shift in the attitudes and values of our society's youth. The Central Park "wilding" attack is an infamous example. The youths accused of raping and nearly killing a young jogger in 1989 said afterwards that "it was fun," (Zinsmeister, 1990). A USA Today editorial (Fox & Pierce, 1994) notes that "The new generation of youngsters is more inclined to resort to violence over trivial issues—a pair of Nikes, a leather jacket, or even a challenging glance" (p. 25). Perhaps the problem can best be summed up by Kaihla, a 17-year-old gang member who responded to a question about his interest in gang membership with the statement, "We like violence, and all that. Violence is nice, man. Honestly." (Came et al., 1989, p. 37).

Sociologists generally link the increase in gang membership to issues concerning social disorganization, cultural deprivation, the formation of subculture and the strength inherent in such subcultures, and the strength obtained from small-group membership (Spergel, 1992). Gang membership also shares many commonalities with racism and other forms of discrimination. Membership opens up new opportunities and allows members to develop an "in-group" and an "out-group," while promoting negative feelings toward the out-group. If the causes of gang membership can be linked to a feeling of alienation and a need for empowerment, then it is not surprising that such membership is increasing at an alarming rate.

Finally, we note the disturbing findings indicating that girls are becoming more involved with violence, not only as victims of violence but as perpetrators. For instance, based on a telephone survey of over 400 teens in Boston, Hausman, Spivak, and Prothrow-Stith (1994) found that although boys are more often involved in violence, almost one fourth of girls also report fighting; black youth report witnessing more violence and being threatened more often, but do not report fighting more. Youths agreed that fighting should be avoided, but acknowledged that they lack knowledge of appropriate behavioral options. Clearly, these data on the rising prevalence of crime and violence point to the urgent need to tackle the complex issues from two directions at once: increased efforts at law enforcement and deterrence, coupled with a long-term commitment to provide opportunities for youth to improve their knowledge of personal risk and alternatives to violence, and to improve their skills related to establishing healthy, nonviolent relationships.

Youths as Direct and Indirect Victims of Violence

The distribution of victimization in our society is not even. We now consider who most of the victims are of violent acts. Violence is particularly hard on those who have the fewest resources to resist or escape—identified ethnic groups, visible minorities, women, children, and youth. Consequently, differences in rates of victimization are not incidental; they cannot be explained by bad neighborhoods or being in the wrong place at the wrong time. Although factors such as poverty and chance do contribute to the risk of victimization, to understand the hows and whys of violence we need to look at dynamics that lie behind the differences in victimization rates. To illustrate this problem we first examine the prevalence of victimization of persons who can be identified on the basis of their race, ethnicity, gender, or sexual orientation.

Violence Against Identified Groups/Minorities

Racial Violence. Despite years of well-intentioned efforts to make integration work there are still marked differences in the status and opportunities of whites and non-whites in North American society. Disturbingly, one quarter of all African American men are in jail, on probation, or on parole, leaving more than 60% of African American children without fathers (Whitaker et al., 1991). Disproportionately high numbers of African Americans drop out of school, and almost 40% of them cannot find jobs (Morganthau, Mabry, Genao, & Washington, 1991). In parallel, visible minorities are still underrepresented in positions of status and responsibility (e.g., according to a poll, 92% of African Americans indicated that they worked for a boss of another race, compared to 42% of whites (Morganthau et al., 1991). African American and Hispanic persons are overrepresented among the poor, and hence make up the vast majority of the population of poor and high-crime inner cities. The obvious connection between such poverty and racial discrimination is a powerful backdrop to the high rates of crime and violence among youth, and something that is an integral concern for planning prevention strategies.

Unfortunately the evolving social structure of our cities and schools is serving to intensify the problem of racially motivated violence. In 1991-1992, two thirds of America's African American students attended schools that were predominantly filled with minority students, leading some to refer to a "new era of segregation." In larger cities, for example, 15 out of every 16 African

American and Hispanic students attend schools where whites are in the minority (Kantrowitz & Wingert, 1993).

At first glance this shift in racial composition could be viewed as a natural way to quell racial tensions. Researchers studying the development of prejudice and stereotypes, however, have highlighted a process referred to as "contact theory," which places prominence on contact, particularly close and sustained contact, with members of different cultural groups. Such ongoing contact promotes more positive, accepting attitudes among persons from diverse racial and cultural backgrounds, and thus is in opposition to planned as well as forced segregation. Individuals with friends of another race, for example, hold fewer stereotypes and more positive views about that race (Ellison & Powers, 1994). Through increasing segregation of public schools the opportunity for young people to understand first-hand the values, lifestyles, and experiences of different racial groups is eliminated, and such ignorance is one of the most fundamental reasons for discrimination and violence.

Sadly, racial tension is high among the young. In 1987-1988, over 70% of those arrested for perpetrating racially motivated crimes in New York State were under the age of 20 (Pinderhughes, 1993). As expressed by a youth from New York: "The police know the blacks don't belong in our neighborhood—everybody knows if they are here they must be looking for trouble. It's up to us to make sure they stay out of our neighborhood" (Pinderhughes, 1993, p. 485). These statements are often backed up by the action of youth gangs that are organized around racial and ethnic boundaries. When interviewing young people about motives behind racially motivated crimes, the young people felt that they were victims of favoritism toward blacks, of reverse discrimination, double standards, and the increasing amount of black power in the city. As one youth put it, "People in my neighborhood don't like how things are going. There aren't enough jobs. You've got all these homeless people. When things get bad, it gets tense, especially when the blacks get all the attention. Except when some black guy gets beat up or something, then everybody's looking at us and calling us racist" (Pinderhughes, 1993, p. 484).

As we will see later on, these are some of the same attitudes that support the backlash related to violence against women—the attitude that women are receiving favoritism and are receiving an inordinate amount of resources to counter their problems, compared to other individuals who suffer from the ills of society. Such a backlash can be seen across a wide segment of North American society, whenever issues related to equality are raised (Swim et al., 1995).

BOX 1.5

"I was walking through Beinecke Plaza late at night with another lesbian. We were walking without actually touching, but our assailants/abusers assumed we were lesbians. A group (4-5) of men approached us and shouted terms of abuse—'dykes,' 'disgusting bitches,' and so forth. Their behavior was threatening and suggested an intended attack" (Yale student quoted in Herek, 1993, p. 19).

Violence Directed Against Gays, Lesbians, and Bisexuals. The extent of violence and abuse levied against persons with different sexual orientations further demonstrates the underlying hatred and ignorance that perpetuates such crimes. In recent surveys, gay, lesbian, and bisexual individuals report being verbally abused (87%); spat on (15%); punched, hit, or kicked (23%); and followed (38%) for intimidation purposes (Berrill, 1990). Based on a sample of undergraduates attending Yale University, for example, Herek (1993) found that lesbian, gay, and bisexual respondents indicated that while they were at the university: 25% had been threatened with physical violence, and 42% experienced some form of physical abuse because of their sexual orientation (e.g., had objects thrown at them, had personal property damaged or destroyed, or had been beaten). More than one third of the sample indicated that fear of attack had caused them to modify their behavior—the young men and women reported that they tried to hide their sexual preferences by monitoring their behavior and speech, not expressing affection in public, and avoiding specific locations and situations where harassment seemed likely.

Similar findings have been reported across other university campuses (see Herek, 1993), suggesting that "coming out of the closet" is indeed a dangerous excursion. Because the vast majority of adolescents are extremely negative toward lesbians and gays (Van de Van, 1995), persons with nontraditional sexual orientation face tremendous challenges in gaining acceptance of their sexual orientation from their peers and family members.

BOX 1.6

Every 15 seconds a woman in the United States is beaten by her husband or boyfriend, and every 6 minutes a woman is forcibly raped (DiCamio, 1993).

Women face only about one third the murder risk of men; however, women are more than four times likely to be murdered by spouses or other intimate partners (Roth, 1994).

Violence Against Women.   Violence against women, in both overt and disguised forms, appears to be occurring at a rate that far surpasses previous estimates. Incidence reports reveal that a married woman is nine times as likely to be killed by her spouse than by a stranger, based on crime data from 1974 to 1992 (Wilson & Daly, 1994). Teenaged wives incur the greatest risk of being killed by husbands, with an increasing age disparity between the man and the woman being associated with a higher risk of homicide.

One of the most thorough and in-depth surveys of violence against women was conducted by Statistics Canada (1993), in which 12,300 randomly chosen Canadian women 18 years of age and over were interviewed by telephone about their experiences with all forms of violence and abuse (ranging from workplace harassment to assault in and outside of the home). The survey found that 29% of these women who have ever been married or lived with a man in a common-law relationship had been assaulted by him on one or more occasions, and that 1 in 10 of the women said that they had been assaulted within the 12 months prior to the poll. Moreover, nearly 1 attack in 5 (18%) was violent enough to injure the woman physically.

Sexual assault of women by their partners or acquaintances was also highlighted by this federally sponsored survey. Extrapolating

from this large sample, researchers estimated that 39% of all women
have experienced at least one incident of sexual assault since age
16, with 24% having experienced the more serious forms of sexual
assault.

Physical and Sexual Assault of Youth

BOX 1.7

Over a 4-month period in Detroit, 102 youngsters ages 16
and under were shot, and nearly all were shot by other
children or youth (Zinsmeister, 1990).

In Baltimore, of 168 teenagers surveyed in an inner-city
clinic for routine medical care, 72% reported knowing
someone who had been shot. The teens themselves had
been victims on average one and a half times and had
witnessed an average of more than five serious criminal
episodes (Zinsmeister, 1990).

Children and youth are too often victims of violence in current
society. Although our media often portrays youth as the perpetrators
of violence, correspondingly less attention has been paid to the
victimization of youth, which has the potential to interfere with the
developmental process in a significant manner.

A recent national telephone sample of 2,000 youth between 10
and 16 years old informs us of the enormity of such victimization
(Boney-McCoy & Finkelhor, 1995). Disturbingly, 35.1% of the
respondents reported experiencing a *completed* victimization at
some point in their lives, and an additional 5.4% reported either an
attempted kidnaping or sexual assault. Female adolescents were
most likely to suffer sexual assault (15.3%), and male adolescents
were most likely to suffer aggravated assault by a nonfamily perpetrator (18.4%).

The impact of these victimization experiences were also documented in the study. Victimized boys and girls reported experiencing more posttraumatic stress disorder (PTSD)-related symptoms
in the past week, more sadness in the past month, and more trouble
with teachers over the past year than nonvictimized respondents.

Both sexual and physical assault had the strongest association with all three of the above adjustment indicators, and acts involving parental violence were associated with marked PTSD-related symptomatology for both genders.

Based on these polled estimates of victimization experiences and their impact, the researchers conclude that 6.1 million youths between 10 and 16 years old, which is more than one third of all youths of this age, have suffered physical or sexual assault. Consequently, these youths are more likely to display elevated signs of distress that includes over a twofold increase in feelings of sadness and difficulties with teachers.

Violence in Adolescent Dating Relationships

Similarly startling statistics have been reported involving dating relationships among young couples. Conservative estimates of prevalence indicate that approximately 35% of women report having been physically assaulted by a dating partner, and 18% of the men state having used physical abuse against a dating partner since leaving high school (DeKeseredy & Kelly, 1993). Furthermore, studies indicate that between 15% and 25% of male college students, and 9% to 39% of high school students engage in some level of physical or sexual aggression toward women (Wolfe, Wekerle, Reitzel-Jaffe, & Gough, 1995).

Among high school students, Sudermann and Jaffe (1993) found more than half of the girls and 30% of the boys (out of a large sample of 1,547 students) reported some form of verbal and emotional abuse by a dating partner. Among 9th and 10th graders, for instance, 40% of the females reported having experienced emotional or verbal abuse from boys that they were casually dating, while 59% report having physical abuse, and 28% sexual abuse in a steady dating relationship.

The degree of acceptance of violence among teens is reflected in Sudermann and Jaffe's (1993) findings that about 20% of male students said that forced intercourse was alright "if he spends money on her," "if he is stoned or drunk," "if they had been dating for a long time." Roscoe's (1985) survey of 126 female college students found a similarly high level of acceptance—70% of the sample listed at least one form of violence as acceptable in a dating relationship, and 80% mentioned a situation in which physical force was tolerable. Although slapping is cited as acceptable most often (49%), punching one's dating partner was seen as acceptable by 21% of the sample. In explaining their choices to use violence, the young women in this survey felt that violence was acceptable in self-defense, to get a partner's attention, and when acting out jealousy. It is also noteworthy that 18% of the women felt violence was acceptable if the couple was "playing," and 17% felt violence was acceptable if their partner was "out of control."

Violence against women in *adult* relationships has been defined by a constellation of behaviors including isolation of self and partner, limiting self and partner's gender roles, controlling/ dominating of partner, expression of jealousy and rage toward the woman, coercive sexual behavior, verbal and psychological abuse, as well as physical assault (Dobash & Dobash, 1992; Walker, 1989). Emerging evidence indicates that violence in adolescent dating relationships mirrors the same processes, incorporating an abuse of power and control over one's partner and an inability or reluctance to leave the abusive partner. Makepeace (1981) first recognized that acts of violence between dating high school students resembles that of college-aged students, which resembles that of married couples. Thus, high school students may be establishing patterns that can persist well into long-term relationships and marriage.

Studies also find that teen victims of violence behave in a manner not unlike that of battered women, that is, they have particular difficulty recognizing their own abuse and leaving abusive relationships. Sadly, only about half of victims terminate the relationship following a violent act, and a significant proportion of those who remain in the relationship report being unaffected by the violence (see Bethke & DeJoy, 1993). Such responses on the part of adolescent girls are understandable in light of the enormous pressure on them to have sexual relations only within the context of a dating relationship (ostensibly to avoid a "bad reputation"; Girshick, 1993).

Socialization of girls is such that they are more likely to believe that they, not males, are responsible for maintaining relationships. Their lack of experience in relationships gives teens little comparison on which to base their decisions, with little or no history of successful actions to take. Moreover, adolescent females often confuse jealousy with love, and are reluctant to turn to adults for help (Girshick, 1993). One can conclude from these findings that some teens are adjusting to violence as a normal course of intimate relationships, which serves as a beginning to an unhealthy pattern of intimate interaction that extends into adulthood.

Although young men and women report being both recipients and perpetrators of dating violence, it is important to highlight gender differences and similarities in terms of motivations for violence, and especially the gender-specific *effects* of such violence. For example, Follingstad, Wright, Lloyd, and Sebastian (1991) found that college-aged female victims were more likely than male victims to attribute physical abuse as "the male trying to get control over them and the male seeking retaliation because she hit him first" (p. 53), whereas males attributed female aggression as "wanting to show how angry they were and as wanting to retaliate for feeling emotionally hurt or mistreated" (p. 53). Male and female perpetrators of physical violence against a partner also differed in terms of their motivations, with female perpetrators using force in retaliation for feeling emotionally hurt, and male perpetrators using force in retaliation for being hit first.

These findings help us to understand that the relatively low-level acts of violence that are commonplace among teen relationships may be a reasonable point of entry for educating young men and women about the abuse of power and control during the formative stages of dating. As the following chapter points out, however, many of the primary ways communities respond to the issue of youth violence are largely reactionary, punitive, and not cost-effective. Because responding to acts of violence and their consequences once they have become known is only a management strategy, the potential to have a lasting impact on violence prevention has not been adequately explored.

CHAPTER TWO

Responding to Violence

BOX 2.1
"Too much money is spent on dealing with young people in the justice system and not enough on teaching them to be healthy and responsible. . . . What we really need is to keep young people from committing acts in the first place. . . . For young people to get the kind of programs they needed, they had to end up in the court system" (National Crime Prevention Council, 1995, quoted from the Internet).

These findings, recently noted by a Canadian federal crime prevention council, reflect the disturbing status of how North American society approaches issues concerning youth. The council visited six regions of the country and found that counselling for drug problems, abuse, or anger control is typically provided *only if a young person is in trouble with the law*. The council further concluded that lack of investment in community programs drives up the costs in the long run because governments spend more on police, courts, and jails. These findings are shocking—certainly not because they are new or revolutionary, but because they are so obvious, straightforward, and consistently ignored.

26

In addressing the needs of youth and attempting to prevent violence in relationships, we need to look closely at the models on which our efforts are based. In general, most efforts to date have been designed as "deficit" models, which assume that the person is a "carrier" of the problem. He or she is therefore viewed as the problem itself, and intervention methods involve treatment of the person directly. Deficit models, although helpful in some respects, are more likely to lead to feelings of blame or rejection of the person with the problem. Such individuals are seen as weak because of their deficits, their ignorance of how to adapt, or both.

Evidence supporting the conclusion that existing programs for stopping violence miss the point and fail to look at violence in the context of a relationship can be seen in our reporting of the problem—much of the focus on violence is between unrelated adults, despite reports that such violence is only a small proportion of the problem. For example, the National Research Council (1993a) indicated that among all homicides in which the relationship between victims and their killers was known by the police (60% of the total), strangers accounted for only 2 in 10, while intimate partners or family members accounted for 3 of every 10, and other acquaintances accounted for 5 of every 10 homicide. Notably, only one fifth of the male victims were murdered by a stranger, and one eighth of the female victims.

By a sizable majority, violent offenders are known to the victim. In many of these cases, moreover, this relationship may in fact be an instrumental component of the violence: the closeness of the relationship, the interdependence of needs, the privacy of the family home, and similar issues related to possible abuse of power and control. Sadly, although women have a lower homicide rate than men, women are four times more likely than men to be killed by their partner.

Despite these findings, the public image of violence continues to focus on the most obvious and extreme cases. These cases are easier to glamorize, and unfortunately often provide the public with the simplistic explanation that such individuals are "deviant." This widely held misconception, that the most visibly violent individuals are the most dangerous and the most deviant, has unfortunately led to the proliferation of treatment and management services that emphasize punitive controls *after the fact*. Because we have no way of detecting and punishing/treating individuals before they have done anything wrong, we leave it up to the natural course of events to determine who should receive the limited services and opportunities we have to offer.

The problem with this approach is obvious—it doesn't work very effectively, and it costs enormous sums of money to attempt to repair the harm to victims or to rehabilitate individuals who are least likely to change or benefit. The economic costs of violence against women, for example, have been estimated at $4.2 billion annually in Canada alone (Greaves, Hankivsky, & Kingston-Riechers, 1995). These costs, which do not take into account the emotional suffering and deterioration of the quality of life, reflect the burden on social services (e.g., shelters, second-stage housing, job training, lost productivity), law enforcement (e.g., police investigations), criminal justice (e.g., prosecution, custody and access), and healthcare. Those who argue that it is too expensive to make a concerted effort to eliminate violence in the family need to take careful note of where the money is actually being spent, and question the extent of the benefit the money is likely to have by that time.

As a case in point, we draw on a recent murder trial in Canada— what has been dubbed Canada's "crime of the century." The defendant pleaded not guilty to two counts of murder of young school-girls, and went to trial. At the trial, videotaped evidence of his sexual assaults, threats, and captivity of the girls was shown, and he was eventually found guilty of the crime after a lengthy and costly trial. Although the North American criminal justice process is one of the best in the world, this investigation and court proceeding cost the taxpayer $11 million—not to mention the $140,000 or so per year it will cost to house this sex offender in a federal prison and offer "treatment" (Kaihla, 1995). This money is spent because of the perception that there is no other choice.

The same day that the verdict was announced, the Ontario provincial government closed the Institute for the Prevention of Child Abuse in Toronto, a group committed for over a decade to educating the public and training professionals about child abuse issues. As this illustrates, we keep limiting our choices, and we fall back on what we know best—punish the offender once he (or she) is proven guilty and hope this deters others.

Deterrence and punishment, however, are more effective when combined with positive alternatives (Gottfredson & Hirschi, 1995). Where does this current strategy, therefore, make room for prevention and planning? As long as we are geared toward detection and containment, all of our resources and talents are drained into that vast cavity. At some point it becomes imperative to "protect" some resources for proactive planning and services that will have a longer term payoff and that might break the seamless cycle of diverting all of our resources toward those who are least likely to benefit.

As a form of introduction to our model of prevention, we take a look at some of the ways our current systems attempt to address the issue of violence. Subsequently, we turn to the significance of adolescent development and interests as one promising avenue for promoting healthy, nonviolent relationships.

The Packaging of
Treatment and Services

Over the years health and social services have become geared to address specific problems, often in isolation and with little regard to the systemic nature of disease and health. If a person is diagnosed as an alcoholic, he or she is sent to an alcohol rehabilitation program. If a couple are having problems with their five-year-old, they are sent to a specialist to discuss behavior management. What has evolved in response to this approach are individually based services offered by separate agencies, with less and less centralized planning and coordination. The visible problems displayed by children and other family members, however, usually are rooted in complex, interconnected ways that often cannot be treated in isolation. Thus, we often have a poor match between the needs of the "consumer" and the available resources being offered.

Despite overlap in needs of children and families, our current services seldom work in a coordinated fashion. Comparing the orientations and practices of child welfare agencies and women's shelters serves as a useful illustration of these opposing roles. Child welfare services are commonly focused on the best interests of the child (i.e., who can keep the child safest). But if a woman cannot protect herself, there are often concerns raised as to her ability to protect her children (Schechter & Edleson, 1994). Thus, child protection workers are often angry at the mother or do not have the time to wait for the mother to straighten out her life. From a child welfare perspective, the cause of the woman's abuse is seen as stress related, in which case supportive services are provided to put the family back on track and work to create a healthy functioning unit. Moreover, she often stays in the home to ensure the necessary financial support for her children.

In contrast, women's groups and shelters are concerned about violence against the woman and how this plays a role in the child's safety and protection. The goals in these settings are to empower their clients and to allow the women to develop strategies for protecting themselves. These organizations may be critical of child protection agencies for placing additional blame on the mother. Their view is that the perpetrator uses violence to exert coercive power and control over other family members, so the intention of the shelter is to provide such oppressed family members with greater power and more options for safety. They often see separation from the perpetrator as a more desirable outcome for both the woman and her children.

The result of these conflicting strategies to service delivery is that people (service providers as well as consumers) often do not recognize the significant role that abuse and violence play in maintaining the status quo in the family. Unless there is visible injury and harm, we are reluctant to approach such sensitive issues as safety, fear, and freedom of choice. When we wait too long to enter into a discussion of sensitive, personal family issues, it is little wonder that family members are practiced at their skill in hiding these issues and protecting one another from such intrusion and uncertainty. We need to make it easier to raise these issues *before* some action becomes imminent and family members are in peril. This becomes less of an issue of family privacy and more one of public awareness, safety, and health for all concerned.

Examining Our Ways
of Caring for Victims

BOX 2.2

"The child welfare system in general, and foster care in particular, is supposed to provide a 'safety net' for children and adolescents who face developmental risks because of dysfunctional families, high-risk neighborhoods, mental health, or behavioral problems. But there is clear evidence that this net has failed, that the child welfare system is doing an inadequate job of preparing the adolescents in its care to make the transition to productive, independent adulthood. For many adolescents who entered its care, the child welfare system has become a high-risk setting" (National Research Council, 1993b, p. 175).

BOX 2.3

"Yesterday's well-intentioned discreet program designed to resolve a particular problem for a particular target group has become part of today's morass of fragmented efforts, which are too often inflexible, narrow, crisis-oriented, and provider driven, and whose available services do not match family needs" (Morrill, 1993, p. 1).

BOX 2.4

"A common sight in public housing developments is a 2- or 3-year-old wandering around without supervision. Nobody cares. Why isn't this youngster in child care? Well, the mother is not working or looking for work. Meanwhile, the child has not been abused and/or neglected badly enough to be declared dependent and eligible for various social programs. The nation is being penny wise and pound foolish again" (Reno, 1994, p. 36).

The Child Welfare System:
"Just in Time" Delivery

Child welfare and foster care have a bleak history. Child welfare services were originally designed for short-term evaluation and placement, with the hope that children would soon be returned home or adopted. But for many it has become a purgatory (Azar, 1995). In any given year, more than 500,000 U.S. children reside in foster care (Morganthau et al., 1994), with infants, toddlers, and preschoolers making up the fastest growing percentage of new placements. Although intended to be short term, less than 40% of children under 10 years of age who remain in care longer than 2 years will ever return home, and 60% of children born to substance abusers and discharged from the hospital to foster care are still there 3 years later (Azar, 1995). The shortage of trained foster parents results in shifting children from one home to the next and often separating siblings (Shealy, 1995). It should come as no surprise, therefore, that 20% of children in runaway shelters come directly from foster care, that children in out-of-home care are at higher risk of developing alcohol and drug problems, and that in Illinois 80% of prisoners spent time in foster homes as children (Azar, 1995).

Although the child welfare system has been the main line of defense in assisting child victims of abuse and neglect (as well as related family crises) for almost a century, we know very little about the effectiveness of this system (Thompson & Wilcox, 1995). Instead, we hear only of its failures, such as the recent shocking death of Elisa Izquiredo after countless interventions by child welfare authorities in New York (Van Biema, 1995). The system was designed to be response-oriented, whereby the worst problems and needs are given highest priority. The focus, therefore, has been on the most visible and personally threatening issues; more systemic influences have to be ignored, such as the economic circumstances of the family, the occurrence of violence by other members in the home, poor housing, and so forth.

It is no secret that the child welfare systems in both the United States and Canada are considered to be a failure. The performance of the system was evaluated by the U.S. Advisory Board on Child Abuse and Neglect (USABCAN; 1991), which concluded that there were emergency needs in every part of the system. Some of these needs are summarized (USABCAN, 1991, p. 15-16) as the following:

1. The child protection system in the United States has a poor sense of mission, and often disregards the needs of children. For example:
   a. the focus is on checking whether parents did or did not act in a certain way, did/did not fulfill a particular service plan (essentially, a continued investigation and detection role);
   b. children themselves often do not receive services that are in any way tailored to their individual needs;
   c. often insufficient attention is given to the relationships that are important to children;
   d. children and youth are not given an active voice in decisions being made about them, and they are often not well-informed about the proceedings that are determining their lives;
2. Increasing numbers of children are living in poverty in communities so drained that individual families often lack support;
3. Resources have failed to grow at a rate anywhere close to the explosive rise in the number of reports of child maltreatment or the complexity of the cases;
4. Interventions that disrupt families are more readily available than those that preserve families in crisis or that prevent serious problems that threaten children's safety and development;
5. Child protection policy is largely unplanned; it has consisted primarily of ad hoc responses to crises.

Costs and Results of
the Child Welfare System

These concerns are magnified by the reality of the costs of this current system. A highly conservative estimate by the General Accounting Office of the costs for mandated services for children who have been abused or neglected, including medical care, family counselling, foster care, and specialized education, is more than $500 million annually in the United States (General Accounting Office, 1991). This estimate is dwarfed, however, by the conclusions of the U.S. Advisory Board on Child Abuse and Neglect (1991):

> Billions of dollars are spent each year in direct expenditures on a child protection system that is failing to protect children adequately. Child

> maltreatment results in costs for law enforcement, the courts, out-of-home care, and the treatment of adults recovering from child abuse. The indirect costs of child maltreatment are even greater . . . the nation continually pays for the social and personal costs of substance abuse, eating disorders, depression, adolescent pregnancy, suicide, juvenile delinquency, prostitution, pornography, and violent crime—*all of which may have substantial roots in childhood abuse and neglect.* (p. 6; italics added)

Given the high cost of this system, is it effective? The problem may not be that alternative placement of children and youth is necessarily bad (especially when a parent is abusive and not amenable to treatment); rather, the problem may be the assumption that such placement is necessarily good or preferable to keeping the child at home and offering other assistance. This assumption simply has not been supported, mostly because child and youth care workers are unable to meet the emotional needs of children in care any better than the original parents (Shealy, 1995).

A longitudinal study conducted by Fanshel, Finch, and Grundy (1990) indicated that in an attempt to redirect adolescents away from juvenile court, the number of youth in foster homes has been increasing. They also found that young people leave foster care lonely, without their families, poorly educated, lacking in social skills, and vulnerable to unemployment, substance abuse, and homelessness (Anthony & Reeves, 1989). Rzepnicki and Stein (1985) further estimate that 20% to 30% of children who are discharged from foster care will eventually reenter the system.

In terms of longer term outcomes of foster care, Shyne and Schroeder (1978) conducted a survey of young adults 2.5 to 4 years after their discharge from foster care. Of these, 54% had returned to live with their extended family members, and they found that high school completion and skills training led to the best outcome among this population. Consistently, youths reported that contact with their family was often the single most important issue leading to long-term success. Children who were visited by family members performed better on measures of intelligence and emotional adjustment, and showed better overall behavior and maturity. Sadly, however, by the end of 5 years the researcher found that over half of the parents stopped visiting their children.

These findings point to the conclusion that our current approach to victims of abuse and neglect, which is broadly represented by the vagaries of out-of-home placement, is not child sensitive or foresightful. Too often, a child must be identified as a "victim" to receive assistance from nonfamily members, which certainly contradicts the underlying intention of child protection or welfare. Resources are squandered until it becomes absolutely necessary to react. This approach is analogous to business management strategies, in which goods are delivered "just in time" in an effort to cut the cost of stocking products and anticipating demand. Unfortunately, with children and families, waiting until the last minute to intervene or assist is often more destructive than doing nothing at all, and certainly falls far short of meeting the best interests of the child.

System Responses to Offenders

BOX 2.5

"Historically U.S. crime policy has remained remarkably consistent, using 'get tough' strategies to fight periodic crime wars. Just as predictable, this policy has failed: Victimization has continued unabated" (Elias, 1993, p. 6).

"Let us reform our juvenile justice program. It makes no sense to prosecute youngsters for a serious crime, place them into a detention facility for 6 months, and then dump them back out into the streets without anything more. Guess what they're going to be doing again in no time flat?" (Fox & Pierce, 1994, p. 26).

The Criminal Justice/Young Offender Systems

When the juvenile system was begun almost 100 years ago in the United States and Canada, it included reform schools and other forms of institutionalization. The prevailing philosophy was that young persons needed to be retrained to get along in society, not merely punished for their failures and kept from society. Thus, there was frequent use of suspended sentences and probationary dispositions that encouraged repayment of the loss (National Research Council, 1993b). As crime has risen, however, the juvenile system has become more and more like the adult penal system, and increasing numbers of young people pass directly from one into the other.

One of the typical reasons or rationales behind the criminal justice system as it applies to young offenders is that youths should be punished for their transgressions to teach them not to do it again. There is, however, substantial evidence to suggest that harsher sentences do not work (Gottfredson & Hirschi, 1995). Although the number of offenders incarcerated has tripled since 1980, the per capita rates of deaths and injuries due to violence continues to grow. Furthermore, sentencing for violent crimes has grown substantially harsher between 1975 and 1989, yet again the number of violent crimes has continued to increase (Roth, 1994).

Not surprisingly, politicians have failed to examine the existing system, and have chosen instead to go for the "quick fix." Juvenile facilities have already imposed discipline on young offenders, yet comprehensive rehabilitation programs focusing on the roots of crime, including abuse, poor education, and family structure, have not received the attention they deserve. As noted by the *Toronto Star*, "throwing troubled kids against a wall of punishment will make law-abiding citizens feel better, but it's not a guarantee of reform" ("Boot camps," 1995).

BOX 2.6

"You can't respect the law when it doesn't respect you. The things I did were about survival. No one ever asked me why I did what I did" (a young woman, cited in the National Crime Prevention Council, 1995, quoted from the Internet).

Costs and Results of the
Criminal Justice/Young Offender Systems

The renewed emphasis on law and order and "get tough" policies for youth crime and delinquency are being exposed as a waste of money. A report prepared by the Canadian federal justice department (Canadian Press, 1995) says taxpayers spend about $240 million a year jailing young people for mostly *minor* crimes. Anthony Doob, a University of Toronto criminologist and psychologist, reports that every 60-day sentence costs roughly $6,000, and "We're not getting anything from all this money" (p. A10).

BOX 2.7

"Canada spends almost $8 billion a year on its courts, police, and prisons, and locks up more criminals than any other developed country except the United States. Yet, the committee lamented, all that money has failed to put a dent in the rate of violent crime. Wouldn't it be better, then, to spend some of that increasingly scarce money on preventing crime—striking at its roots as Thoreau would say—rather than on punishing criminals?" (Yakabuski, 1994, p. C4).

It is apparent that when it comes to building prisons more is never enough, despite the preponderance of evidence to suggest, after two decades of "law and order politics," that building (and filling) more prisons is not effective at deterring crime (Gottfredson & Hirschi, 1995). It is startling to consider that in 1991 the United States spent $26 billion to build and run prisons and care for those *1.1 million* individuals on probation and parole. The vast majority of these individuals were men. That same year less than $23 billion was spent for the *33.5 million* recipients on aid to families with dependent children (AFDC). The vast majority of these individuals were women and children ("Prison spending," 1993).

Corrections has clearly become a growth industry in the United States: Spending increased 232% for all states and local governments between 1970 and 1990 (yet, 40 states are still under court order or consent decrees to reduce overcrowding; Fox & Pierce, 1994). It is also evident that government spending on the justice system is increasing at a rate that far surpasses spending in other areas. Government spending on the justice system reached $9.57 billion in Canada in 1994 after adjusting for inflation, which represents a 13% increase over 5 years. Youth custody and community service costs also increased by 16% after adjusting for inflation (from $355.9 million in 1988-1989 to $484.9 million in 1992-1993) over a 5-year period (Young, 1994).

If there was an established lack of effective treatment or prevention alternatives for violent juvenile offenders, perhaps retributive, punitive dispositions would have more appeal. A level of sophistication has been achieved, however, in the delivery of such services to show measurable change in violent adolescents, although the endurance of these changes remains unproven (Tate, Reppucci, & Mulvey, 1995). Treatment programs that work may be much less costly than correctional facilities. In 1992, it cost an average of $105.27 per day to keep a juvenile in a correctional facility in the United States, compared to $31.43 per day for multisystemic therapy (Tate et al., 1995). When compared to the cost (roughly $450/year) to deliver early childhood intervention or treatment that is known to reduce the incidence of crime and delinquency (Huether, 1995), the continuation of a massive build-up of correction facilities seems very shortsighted.

Changing Course: Building Healthy Relationships as a Violence Prevention Strategy

Like many other social problems, violence can be "graded" from lesser to greater significance. "Minor" acts of violence are so commonplace that they could be considered "normative" behavior, that is, many adolescents and young adults engage in these behaviors at some level in the context of sports, driving an automobile, spanking a child, and so on. Although many adolescents may engage in some degree of antisocial behavior (Hamburg, Millstein, Mortimer, Nightingale, & Petersen, 1993), most do not cause significant harm to themselves or others, and would not be considered a major concern for law enforcement or mental health. The question thus becomes: *Is there a critical point to intervene or assist youth and their families that will have the greatest benefit, or must we wait for the problem to be clearly identified first?*

The "disease model" of physical health has contributed a great deal to our understanding of diseases and disease processes. Consequently, it is not surprising that this method was adopted when looking for ways to understand broader social issues. That is, much of the mental health movement rests on the assumption that a deviant target population exists, and therefore shifts in program emphasis are often based on what is perceived to be a better state of affairs. Unfortunately, very little empirical evidence is available to assist in such decisions. A disease model assumes that to prevent an illness from occurring it is necessary first to establish its etiology or cause in full. As well, it presumes that a person either has a disease or does not, and we either treat the person or we do not.

This analogy, however, does not extend well to social problems. In the case of social illnesses, there are often many patterns of behavior or at-risk indicators that precede the actual occurrence of the behavior, whether it be a criminal behavior or some other deviant or undesirable behavior (Jessor, 1993). A disease-based paradigm not only fails to identify individual strengths, but it also disempowers the very individuals we need to motivate to affect change. Thus, instead of focusing attention on ways of identifying and diagnosing pathologies, we need to develop the tools for eliciting and channeling strengths and talents of youth to help them adapt successfully, especially in ways that match their needs and interests long before failure sets in.

In contrast to the deviation and disease models described here, a health promotion model is predicated on the grounds that efforts to assist others must be *inclusive*, rather than *exclusive*. Such a model builds on strengths, rather than attempting to treat known weaknesses alone. Within the framework of a health promotion model, it is often more useful to look for the "at-risk" indicators and reduce their potency, than to wait for the person to show the undesired behavior. On one hand, because most forms of violence occur within the context of a close or intimate relationship, we have progressed considerably in terms of identifying preexisting risk factors that are amenable to change or elimination (as discussed in Chapter 5). Yet, on the other hand, our policies and actions still remain overly focused on the discovery of deviancy within the individual that will account for the tremendous expected differences between "them" and "us."

Thus, there may be some advantage to changing our emphasis more toward what we *want to encourage*, while still maintaining clarity and principles concerning what we want to prevent. Beyond the simple notion of what constitutes violence, we need to consider the definition of *healthy, nonviolent relationships*. Violence and nonviolence are not polar opposites, but rather end-points of a broad range of more desirable or less desirable interpersonal behaviors, some of which society has specifically declared as illegal and deserving of "intervention." The advantage of viewing violence in this manner is that it helps us to recognize that certain acts do not have to cross an arbitrary "threshold" before they would be labeled as violent or abusive. We can choose to define our own threshold, irrespective of legal definitions, to encourage young people to recognize that a verbally or physically abusive act toward another person (for example) is not judged as wrong on the basis of whether the person complained, whether the act was witnessed, or whether the offender was caught. We prefer, instead, to promote behavior that is much less often talked about, taught, or even considered—to promote *nonviolence*.

Whereas most of us are familiar with using the term "violence" to refer to particular acts of intention and harm, we have given less thought to what constitutes *nonviolence* (Earls, Cairns, & Mercy, 1993). The implications are significant: If we focus our attention and resources only on the occurrence of undesirable behavior (i.e., violence), we are likely to seek ways to prevent its occurrence through means of identification, control, and punishment. If, however, we look at the other side of the equation, the promotion of healthy, nonviolent relationships, we seek ways to

- Establish and build trust
- Share thoughts, ideas, and feelings
- Respect each other's thoughts, ideas, and feelings
- Encourage and support each other to grow
- Permit each person to feel loved and valued
- Ensure that each person feels safe to express disagreement and negative feelings including anger, disappointment, frustration, and so on
- Ensure that each person feels safe when another person expresses disagreement and negative feelings

This shift in perspective opens us up to a completely different list of intervention and educational possibilities, most of which have little to do with punishing offenders after the fact. These possibilities include school-based educational curricula (see Sudermann, Jaffe, & Hastings, 1995), neighborhood-based health and social services (Barry, 1994; Garbarino & Kostelny, 1994), family-based childcare and health care (Olds, in press), and individually based efforts to enhance skills, knowledge, and actions (the primary foci of this book).

BOX 2.8
What 100 youths said they needed most:

- Meaningful chances to learn, work, and play;
- A life free of abuse and neglect;
- A voice in helping reduce crime and violence;
- Positive role models;
- Fair, clear, and consistent consequences if they do something wrong (National Crime Prevention Council, 1995).

In addition to an effective criminal justice response, a viable strategy to reduce violence against women and children begins with a view that youth are not merely targets of intervention but part of a planned approach. Youth need to learn more about power and status, to avoid such abuses in the future. Educational and cultural experiences in which power is understood and not abused would assist in this manner. Recognition of their inherent status and how such status may easily be abused is also critical.

Youth, especially high-risk youth, need education and skills to promote healthy relationships, to develop peer support, and to establish social action aimed at ending violence in relationships. The most effective prevention programs empower young people to be involved in the work, which then becomes rewarding through the promotion of cooperation and mutual support.

Adolescence represents a crucial link in the prevention of violence in relationships. It is an important time for relationship formation, and it is also a period in which the scars of childhood or inadequate opportunities for adaptation can impair normal adjustment. The passive choice would be to continue addressing the needs of youth in an inconsistent, reactionary manner. The active choice involves a new paradigm committed to the needs and resources of youth.

CHAPTER THREE

Establishing a Commitment to Violence Prevention

BOX 3.1

"Methods of identifying and diagnosing the pathologies of youth are finely honed, but our tools for eliciting and channeling the strengths and talents of youth are either blunt or nonexistent. Our approach to youth must be rethought, because our current practices are not working" (Calhoun, 1992, p. 334).

Retracing Our Steps: From Discovery to Prevention

Unlike modern society, ancient Chinese society defined its orientation to medicine and healing based on its views of ways to encourage health and growth rather than eliminating disease. The Chinese viewed health as a state of dynamic balance between the interrelated biological, psychosocial, and environmental components that determine human performance (Millstein, Petersen, & Nightingale, 1993). From this viewpoint or paradigm, "illness" represented an imbalance, which could be caused by personal factors (such as diet or exercise), disharmonies in the family, or lack of skills/resources to meet the demands of living effectively. This rather simple view was one of the earliest known "ecological perspectives" on human health and behavior, because it considered the human organism within the context of social and environmental influences. "Health" was seen as a worthy and appropriate goal, comprised of much more than just the "absence of illness."

Anglo-Saxon culture has viewed "health" and "illness" quite differently than the above examples, due in large part to the major developments in medicine that occurred during the later part of the 19th century. The discovery of "germ theory" and the successful treatment of infectious diseases strengthened the emerging belief that illness and disease were evidence of biological problems— hence, the absence of such illness was considered to be evidence of health (Millstein et al., 1993).

A similar history can be traced concerning how we have dealt with problems of children and youth (this history, however, is very poorly recorded prior to the 18th century; see Levine & Levine, 1970). In colonial times, "intervention" for problem children or youths was simple and largely "effective"—abandonment, imprisonment, long-term hospitalization, or even death for unruliness (by virtue of the Massachusetts "Stubborn Child Act," although no sentences were reportedly carried out). By the mid-1800s troubled children and youth were mainly described in reference to mental retardation (fools, idiots) and, like disturbed adults, were to be distrusted and scorned as the work of the "devil" and similar evil forces.

Initial (albeit naive) optimism emerged briefly during the mid-19th century (based on what has been termed the "cult of curability" through institutions for the insane; Achenbach, 1982), as the "feebleminded" were distinguished from the insane and placed in special training schools. This early educational model for the retarded, however, soon returned to a custodial (management) model and, by the turn of the 20th century attitudes toward the retarded had turned from pessimism to hostility and disdain. An "alarmist period" ensued, in which mentally retarded children, youth, and adults were blamed for most crime and social ills. Disturbingly, segregation and sterilization became the intervention of choice (Deutsch, 1949).

The "first generation" of change in thinking was led by the recognition of major psychological disorders and the formulation of a taxonomy of illnesses. Such recognition served to organize and categorize ways to identify various problems of children and adults, which gave some semblance of understanding and control. This shift in perspective and knowledge also prompted the development of diagnostic categories, new criminal offenses, expanded descriptions of deviant behavior, and added more comprehensive monitoring procedures for identified individuals.

The Mental Hygiene Movement, spearheaded by Clifford Beers (a mentally disturbed layperson who recovered his faculties and worked to change the plight of others so afflicted) was founded in 1909, sought to *prevent* mental disease by raising the standards of care and disseminating reliable information. As a result, detection and intervention methods began to flourish, based on a more tempered, yet still quite frightened and ill-informed, view of afflicted individuals. This paradigm, however, was largely based on a disease model, and therefore intervention was limited to those with the most visible and prominent disorders.

The next generation in the development of our approach to children and youth involved greater study of the early precursors and causes of deviant behavior, violent behavior, and similar irregularities, in an attempt to predict who would be violent or abused and to assist in treatment of the afflicted. Therapeutic models grew rapidly, along with studies showing the significance of individual, family, peer, and cultural influences on such behavior. New social programs emerged, based on the notion that early intervention might bolster one's chances of resisting the known forces that create abnormal behavior. This view spawned the community mental health movement, which for the first time began to credit the "patient" (or "client") with some ability to remain as a contributing member of society. Terms such as "primary prevention," "early intervention," and "community action" appeared, and a growing optimism was felt concerning the ability of modern psychiatry, psychology, and social work to identify and remove the impediments to mental health (Levine, 1981). Although this movement was a dramatic shift away from disease, it borrowed heavily from the public health model, which was largely one of *protection from disease* rather than promotion of health.

The third, and current, generation of research and thinking added to the second the idea that disorders come in "clusters," with overlapping etiologies and clinical presentation. On the positive side, this addition to knowledge and understanding helped to recognize the multicausal nature of many child and adult psychological disorders and the importance of contextual factors (e.g., Jessor, 1991); unfortunately, however, the implementation of this knowledge in the field has fallen far short of what was intended.

Rather than striving to remove the major causal agents that lead to multidimensional disorders, it would appear that on many fronts we have chosen instead to become more "efficient." Politically controlled financial priorities dictate how we respond to youth today, and the preference seems to be more on management and containment, to the greater exclusion of proactive efforts at planning and prevention. From a resource perspective a problem has to be visible, clear-cut; and well-established, severe, or both before action can be taken. Management and treatment have prevailed, based on the premise that it is too expensive, unproductive, unimportant, or all of these to provide ways of promoting resistance.

Half Empty or Half Full?

Notably, the contemporary focus on efficiency and priority clashes with opportunities to promote healthy relationships and to value the contribution of youth, instead of looking for what's there, we prefer to look for what's missing. Despite our concern, we (as a society) appear to be locked into a view of the issues faced by youth as being somehow antagonistic to the issues of society at large. Lacking a theory or well-stated paradigm as guidance, too often this perspective relies on unexamined slogans and catchphrases of politically driven repair programs that emphasize an adversarial, "get tough" approach (e.g., career criminals, boot camps, drug testing, "intermediate sanctions," gang units, increased prison terms, and so forth; Gottfredson & Hirschi, 1995). The blame for such problems is shifted entirely onto those individuals who are the most visible offenders and undesirables, and in the process we lose an important opportunity to connect with those who we might reach—those who are younger, with less power and more social disadvantage.

The various paradigms operating on our private and public perspectives of youth can be summarized in the following table. One should note that our approach to youth, therefore, is intricately connected to how we view our primary concern. Our views, however, are more often implicit or poorly visualized, rather than explicit and well-defined. Look, for example, at Table 3.1.

TABLE 3.1

If Our Primary Concern Is:	Then Our Approach to Problems of Youth Would Involve:
a. Safety and public concern	a. Detection, police visibility, increased arrests
b. Cost	b. Reduce services except to those in most dire need
c. Efficiency	c. Adopt service models that are crisis oriented, short term, management focused
d. Protection of youth	d. Crisis lines, alternative care placements
e. Protection of society	e. Increased jail sentences, "tougher" laws, "boot camps"
f. Deviant behavior/mental illness	f. Improved mental health screening and psychiatric services
g. *Health promotion/ empowerment, leadership, competence*	g. Opportunities to enhance self-concept; build awareness and skills that foster healthy, nonviolent relationships

Accordingly, we would like to suggest a further conceptual shift—a fourth generation if you will—that is emerging among an increasingly larger segment of both physical and mental health professionals: Rather than focusing on efficiency, costs, safety, protection, or deviance, this perspective places a high emphasis on health promotion and empowerment, that is, encouraging new changes, opportunities, and competence to achieve one's health potential (Millstein et al., 1993). By definition, this perspective speaks to the importance of attaining a balance between the abilities of the individual (or groups of individuals) and the challenges and risks of the environment.

The implications of these conceptual shifts on the field of medicine are far-reaching: how individuals think about health; how daily life is organized and experienced; and, importantly, the development of social policy, allocation of social resources, and identification of persons to implement these policies. The impact on the field of mental health, and children and youth in particular, has been suggested but not achieved (Takanishi, 1993). We return to the many ways that this perspective can benefit children and youth throughout the remaining chapters.

Overcoming Barriers
to Innovative Solutions

Youth Have Problems, Not Solutions

Adolescence is a time of considerable choices, and the importance of relationship formation has been largely underplayed in relation to violence prevention and health promotion. Instead, solutions to problems of youth violence and youth conflict tend to have over-focused on youth as the cause, with detection and punishment as the solutions. The most prominent philosophy guiding much of the criminal justice and child welfare legislation today is that youth should be controlled and forced to respect authority, that laws should be tighter, and that young offenders should be treated by the criminal justice system as adults. It is not surprising, therefore, that young people have always felt overly criticized and disempowered.

The issue of how adults' perceptions and labeling of children and youths can become biased can be understood when one examines the recent literature on how stereotypes and prejudice are formed and lead to categorical judgments about groups of individuals. Unless these negative perceptions are countered by accurate and attractive alternatives, we will continue to disenfranchise young people and view them more as the problem and not enough as the solution.

As previously noted, society currently operates on a deficit-based, "pathological" model of the problems experienced by and caused by youth. Without due recognition of this simplified interpretation and labeling process we often fail to value what youths may have to offer. Instead, they are seen as the genesis of the problems that adults have identified and want to stop. An example of this "negative bias" toward youth can be seen in an interesting study by Hedin, Hannes, and Saito (1985), in which the researchers first asked elementary school-aged children to describe what they believe adults think of them, both positive and negative. At this younger age, these children felt that adults perceived them to be somewhat disruptive (e.g., "mischievous, pesty, noisy, sassy, clumsy"), but they still felt accepted and valued. By the time they reached adolescence, however, they believed that most adults think of them largely as troublemakers (e.g., "druggies, sex maniacs, rowdies, delinquents, hateful, no good, worthless"), despite their own self-appraisals as being responsible, "more good than bad," and so forth.

Critically, this common practice of applying labels to "targets" (e.g., *homosexual, teenager, homeless*) often influences how we subsequently judge and evaluate similar members of the target group—for example, a push or shove may be seen as more aggressive when it is believed to have come from an African American than from a white male (Duncan, 1976). Two important processes underlie the formation of such biases and discrimination, and both are amenable to change.

We have recognized for some time the significant role of *stereotypes*, which refer to the perceiver's cognitive schemas (i.e., judgments, beliefs, awareness, and so on) about social groups. Because stereotypes are built from cognitive processes they reflect much of our condensed knowledge of a target group—our expectations, beliefs, hypotheses, personality attributions, and so on. It follows, therefore, that a person's stereotypes provide a "short-cut" to interpreting new or unfamiliar situations; that is, he or she is more likely to interpret an ambiguous situation (involving a youth, for example) in ways that are consistent with his or her beliefs about youth (our "intuitive base rates"; Jussim, Nelson, Manis, & Soffin, 1995). Moreover, such stereotypes and prejudice are seductive because they reduce the complexity of an issue, channel our diffuse anxiety toward a particular target or targets, and provide justification for our social policies (such as removing children and youth from their homes; Shealy, 1995).

In conjunction with stereotypes, however, biased perceptions of others also emerge from *prejudices*—the strong affective predispositions we have toward certain groups (positive as well as negative). Not only may we hold strong beliefs about certain target groups, we also may have strong feelings of like or dislike, or attitudes of favor or disfavor, which influence our judgments and behavior toward members of those groups. As shown by Jussim et al. (1995), when perceivers evaluated samples of behavior that they thought were from an identifiable group (i.e., homosexuals or heterosexuals, rock musicians or child abusers), their judgments were strongly influenced by how much they liked the target group, as well as how disturbed they believed persons from such groups to be.

The implications for these studies on policy and program planning warrant attention. It is too easy to become locked into a perspective or paradigm for addressing the problems of youth without a close awareness or tacit understanding, or with certain predispositional feelings that lead to hasty judgments. By examining our stereotypes and prejudices we avoid perpetuating false beliefs, poorly matched solutions, or even destructive policies that are well intended but perhaps misguided. Moreover, research on stereotypes and prejudice informs us that adolescence may be a particularly opportune time to prevent the rigid formation of biases that become the future basis for sexist, racist, homophobic, and similar behaviors.

Providing youths with more accurate knowledge about identifiable groups may be a useful, although insufficient, means of eliminating biases that have a cognitive source (e.g., true base rates of mental illness among certain groups, accurate information about male violence toward women). In addition to knowledge, it is important to address affectively-based sources of prejudice and discrimination that contribute toward negative feelings and hostile attitudes (Jussim et al., 1995). Increasing contact among in- and out-group members appears to be one of the most powerful means of decreasing such affectively-based discrimination, and one that we return to in our discussion of the Youth Relationships Project.

Management or Empowerment?

BOX 3.2

"Creating a useful crisis is part of what this will be about.
So the first bunch of communications that the public might
hear might be more negative than I would be inclined to
talk about (otherwise). Yeah, we need to invent a crisis and
that's not an act just of courage, there's some skill
involved." (The Honorable John Snobelen, Minister of
Education for Ontario; "Are school boards," 1995, p. A3).

Our societal prerogative today is to "manage" youth, in a misguided effort to get past the crisis or conflict "stage" and prevent
them from breaking the rules. Such a management strategy may, to
a certain degree, be a necessary response to the crises and problems
that occur on a daily basis in every town and city. Yet, this response
should not limit us from looking forward to designing something
new, something that might offer an important change in direction
either now or in the near future. It is time to look at how we spend
our time.

In his widely read book on leadership style, Covey (1989) describes how most of us manage our time in a nonproductive,
nonvisionary manner. Drawing a quadrant based on the intersec-
tion of two important dimensions, the degree of "urgency" and the
degree of "importance," Covey demonstrates the four basic ways we
may choose to use (or fail to use) our time (see Table 3.2).

Too often we are consumed by issues that fall within the "urgent,
but not important" category. Phone calls, messages, memos, and
reports demand our "immediate attention," leaving less time for
planned activities. Of course, some of these activities are also very
important and thus warrant our undivided attention ("urgent/
important" category—such as deadlines, meetings, interviews, and
so on). And, like it or not, we all indulge ourselves in the third
quadrant comprised of not urgent, not important "stuff" (like trying
out new computer software, cleaning out our file drawers, and

TABLE 3.2

	Urgent	Not Urgent
Important	I ACTIVITIES: Crises Pressing problems Deadline-driven projects	II ACTIVITIES: Prevention Relationship building Recognizing new opportunities Planning, recreation
Not Important	III ACTIVITIES: Interruptions, some calls Some mail, some reports Some meetings Proximate, pressing matters Popular activities	IV ACTIVITIES: Trivia, busy work Some mail Some phone calls Time wasters Pleasant activities

SOURCE: Covey, S. R. (1989). *The seven habits of highly effective people: Powerful lessons in personal change.* New York: Simon & Schuster. Reprinted with permission.

catching up on events). Notwithstanding these patterns or habits that we develop, to become more effective at whatever our goal may be (i.e., work, relationships, even recreation) it is necessary to develop and build on those activities that fall within the "important, but not urgent" category—creating ways to fulfill our goals, establish important connections, and become proactive at meeting our objectives (Covey, 1989).

Unfortunately, when you consider what youth workers, supervisors, and even government policy planners are occupied with during much of their day, it is apparent that a large discrepancy exists between what most feel is needed and what actually occurs. Much of the time spent today on issues pertaining to children and youth falls within the "urgent/important" quadrant, which leaves very little opportunity for activities that the individual feels relate to his or her effectiveness and strategies to develop innovative solutions.

We have evolved into a pattern of *crisis management,* choosing or being forced to wait until it is absolutely necessary before making any attempt at intervention or reform. Parenthetically, notable exceptions to this pattern include some aspects of medicine, education, and similar services aimed primarily at the healthy, non-problematic majority of the population. Persons who work with troubled youth, therefore, too often are left with a task *that is beyond the capabilities of our current system and resources,* too little, too late, resulting in the well-known signs of stress, burn-out, and fatigue from "putting out fires." This brings us to our next question:

Is Prevention Unrealistic and Too Costly?

The history of efforts to reduce the prevalence of mental health problems in North America has been largely one of treating or punishing recognizable problems in individuals after they have arisen (Levine, 1981). Other than academic interests, there has been little commitment or sustained interest in proactive prevention strategies that view problems shown by individuals as resulting from inadequate resources and coping abilities in relation to their environmental stressors.

In contrast, for most of this century professional groups and government policies have produced incentives (such as training opportunities, third-party payments, and civil suits) that have encouraged a model of intervention based on disease or deviation (i.e., the "medical model") rather than enhancement or support (Levine & Levine, 1970). This perspective still dominates not only because of the entrenched systems and methods that allow for intervention only once the problem has clearly surfaced; in addition, some argue, society is obligated to provide care for those who are most needy, and resources devoted to uncertain efforts at prevention will subtract from the scarce pool of resources available to service the known offenders or the most troubled (Lamb & Zusman, 1979).

Furthermore, critics ask whether it is foolhardy to endorse prevention, especially when the number of known "disease agents" is growing at an exponential rate. We believe it is foolhardy not to do so. Adolescents typically explore potentially damaging activities tentatively, to "try them on for size" (Hamburg, Millstein, Mortimer, Nightingale, & Petersen, 1993, p. 386). Thus, before these negative patterns are firmly established there is a critical and often neglected opportunity for intervention to *prevent* casualties that carry forward across the lifespan. Violence researchers Earls, Cairns, and Mercy (1993) offer a succinct reply to the need for alternative solutions to youth violence and related problems despite the obstacles.

> The obstacles of easy availability of and access to guns, widespread use of alcohol and drugs, the decay of central city areas, and high cultural tolerance for violence cannot be minimized in any campaign to promote nonviolence among today's youth. In the face of these barriers, efforts in health promotion to decrease violent encounters may be equivalent to trying to control an epidemic of tuberculosis in a densely populated area without adequate sanitation. Antibiotics may be of some value in treating individual cases, and a vaccine would be of even greater value in protecting some groups of individuals, but the environmental conditions that promote the disease would simply overwhelm public resources in combating it through these means alone. . . . What we need to promote nonviolence as a health objective is something analogous to what was needed to control infectious diseases toward the end of the last century: vast environmental and policy changes." (p. 296)

Despite its uncertainties, from time to time communities, agencies, and professionals acknowledge that prevention has an appeal that cannot be met by treatment alone. This appeal is supported by three primary considerations (Levine & Perkins, 1987). First, based on our current definitions of deviance and disease, we are recognizing that there will never be enough trained professionals or enough police and prisons to meet the mental health and criminal justice needs of most communities. Second, there continues to be dissatisfaction with the effectiveness of mental health, child welfare, and criminal justice interventions that seek to remove pathology, at-risk children, or dangerous persons in an effort to restore balance, especially in the face of more appealing strategies aimed at enhancing competence, adaptiveness, and similar positive conditions (Albee, 1980).

Finally, prevention may be much more cost-effective than treatment or arrest/incarceration (Kazdin, 1993). For example, the Home Visitation Program is an early intervention program aimed at young, disadvantaged mothers who are at an increased risk of child abuse and neglect. Based on three clinical trials in Elmira, New York; Memphis, Tennessee; and Denver, Colorado, a detailed cost analysis has been conducted (Olds, Henderson, Phelps et al., 1993). The experimental group and control group were compared on the basis of the cost of the following government services during the first 4 years of the child's life: aid to families with dependent children (AFDC), food stamps, Medicaid, child protective services, and foster care. In addition, researchers calculated differences in government revenues generated by income taxes from the women's participation in the workforce. The experimental group started with a deficit, because the service to participants was estimated to cost $1,280/year each. Even taking this deficit into account, however, the experimental group realized a savings of $3,300 in government services per family over the comparison group.

We also acknowledge that although prevention programs are, in general, desirable and effective, some programs are more successful than others. Reviews of the literature reveal particular components of programs that show particular success (see Chapter 6). In general, prevention programs are most effective when they target high-risk individuals before they become involved in risk behaviors, and offer them high-quality programs that are firmly based in theory; in addition, the more integrated and comprehensive the program is, the more likely it is to show success. Problems usually come in packages, and programs that acknowledge this reality and incorporate it into their programs tend to be more successful.

As a summary and integration of the concepts in this chapter, we provide a basic comparison of the goals and target populations for programs described as: (a) Treatment, (b) Prevention, or (c) Promotion (see Table 3.3).

In basic terms, prevention is any effort to stop a problem before it occurs. As such, prevention falls between treatment and promotion on a continuum of service provision. Treatment efforts target the "dysfunctional" population, that is, those individuals who are already experiencing a particular problem, and aims to eliminate that problem. Promotion efforts are aimed at the population in general, and focus on the development of strengths. Prevention efforts are similar to treatment efforts to the degree that they target a particular population; however, instead of targeting a "problem" population, prevention efforts generally target the population that is presently symptom-free but may be "at-risk" for developing

TABLE 3.3 A Hypothetical Continuum of Service Provision

Treatment	Prevention	Promotion
Goal: Eliminate/ control the problem once it has been identified	Reduce the risk of the problem developing	Develop strengths to bolster resistance and increase competence
Target population: Persons with diagnosed or recognized disorders	Persons who may be at risk of developing a disorder	All individuals in the selected population

problems in the future. Prevention efforts strive to reduce the number or magnitude of "risk" in an individual's environment, and to strengthen individual's abilities to combat the challenges that may lead to disorder.

Regardless of these considerable attractions, however, prevention or health promotion have not been popular strategies among professionals or the public when it comes to addressing problems of children and youth. This state of affairs perhaps exists because prevention requires policymakers and administrators to confront social and political factors that undermine lasting solutions to social problems (Levine, 1981).

Prevention entails environmental and cultural factors in addition to individual explanations for the causes of violence and similar concerns, and a strong commitment to large-scale, proactive intervention using public resources rather than individually focused, private interests. Furthermore, prevention requires social and political action directed at achieving fundamental change. Nevertheless, we owe it to children, youth, and families to consider building other bridges that promote competency and adaptive behavior, in an effort not only to prevent something unwanted but also to bolster potential and growth for individuals and society.

CHAPTER FOUR

Approaching Solutions

Youth as Resources

BOX 4.1
"Unfortunately, too few adults invest personal time and effort to encourage, guide, and befriend young people who are struggling to develop the skills and confidence necessary for a successful and satisfying adult life. Too few communities encourage and recognize community service by young people. And too few offer programs and activities to promote healthy adolescent development . . . as a result, many young people believe that they have little to lose by dropping out of school, having a baby as an unmarried teenager, and committing crimes" (Emery, 1993, p. 6).

Adolescent Development: A Good Fit

A number of developmental issues during adolescence make this a particularly significant period for education concerning nonviolence in relationships. Eccles et al. (1993) emphasize that problems in adolescence have an early beginning involving issues of autonomy and control with family members, particularly concerning family decision-making processes. Self-esteem plays a role in how well each adolescent will negotiate these developmental tasks, and it is acknowledged that adolescents need to be a part of the solution for problems related to family decision making to be successfully resolved.

Emotional dependency on parents is relinquished in favor of dependency on peers and, notably, gender differences in the development of such autonomy are common; that is, girls show greater emotional autonomy with respect to their parents than do boys, and girls have more resistance to peer influence (Hill, 1992). Teens must develop the ability to balance the demands of their peer group with the demands of family, and learn to extend and differentiate their social networks (rather than exchange them from home) in accordance with the type of support needed.

Motivation to Learn About Relationships

Clearly, adolescence is a time of important physical changes that youth must learn to understand and regulate, such as changes in sexual motivation and appearance, as well as hormonal changes that may affect anger and mood. Because of the number of physical and psychological changes, this developmental period is a particularly sensitive time for the formation of attitudes and beliefs concerning interpersonal relationships and the abuse of power and control. Most notably, teens are developing an increased interest in sex, which makes them particularly attentive to any issues involving gender, sexuality, and relationship formation.

Adolescence is also a time of important cognitive and social development in which individuals learn to think more rationally and become capable of thinking hypothetically. Adolescents can consider extended time perspectives, not just the here and now, and adjust their goals and behavior accordingly; however, processing of information is still less systematic than formal, and will depend on their prior knowledge and understanding. Thus, it is emblematic that their ability to consider and understand emotionally arousing topics is less sophisticated than that of adults. At the same time they must develop and use effective decision-making skills involving complex interpersonal relationships. These skills include an awareness of possible risks and considerations of future consequences, balancing their own interests with those of their peers, family members, and dating partners.

Self-identity and self-esteem also change dramatically during adolescence. Self-esteem reflects the person's judgment of his or her personal competence across such domains as attractiveness, acceptance by others, and academic, athletic, and interpersonal success. Self-identity, in turn, becomes more solidified as young adults develop a coherent picture of their capabilities and limitations, and select and commit to their personal choices related to sexual, occupational, and social roles.

In parallel, teens develop greater capability for abstract thought, which enables them to formulate a more complex view of themselves, coupled with greater self-reflection, social comparison, and autonomous decision making (Crockett & Petersen, 1993). Harter (1990), however, points out that these important changes are accompanied by certain vulnerabilities. Teens' overestimates of their confidence may lead to failure, whereas underestimates of their own confidence may lead to the avoidance of challenge and a diminished opportunity for growth. Optimally, teens should have the opportunity to explore a wide range of possible options in these domains before having to make commitments to their own identity.

Motivation for Autonomy and Intimacy

Adolescents are starting to make their own decisions about important issues affecting their lives. Self-reliance, self-control, and independent decision making all increase during the teen years, with a shift away from the family and onto the peer group. To the frustration of many parents, conformity to parental opinions gradually decreases while at the same time the tendency to be swayed by peers increases in early adolescence before it declines (Crockett & Petersen, 1993).

Erikson (1950), in his classic lifespan model of psychosocial development, documented that cultural expectations focus youths' energy on two broad developmental tasks: (a) separating from family and making a commitment to an independent identity, and

(b) merging that identity with others in intimate relationships. Those individuals who have clear ideas of their own personal identity may be ready to focus on intimacy goals related to sharing, closeness, and trust in their social dating relationships. For those who are still struggling to assert independence from family and who are experimenting with different identities or selves, social dating goals may revolve around establishing such an identity (Sanderson & Cantor, 1995).

Important gender differences are also emerging during adolescence. Girls report feeling worse about themselves than do boys, in particular around their psychological self-image. Over 40% of girls say they frequently feel ugly and unattractive, and see themselves more positively with respect to interpersonal relations and social ability (Offer & Ostrov, 1981). In contrast, boys see themselves more positively with respect to achievement, academic aspirations, self-assertion, and body image. Males also value control and perceive themselves as more willing to take on leadership roles and responsibilities, whereas females tend to value relationship involvement, social relationships, and a desire of more affection, intimate personal relationships, and for others to initiate more positive personal relationships with them (Bakken & Romig, 1992).

For autonomy to develop, however, young people require opportunities to develop and exercise their autonomy while minimizing risks of negative consequences. To reduce such risks, they need to be well-informed of the possible consequences of various actions, they need to have opportunities to practice alternative perspectives, they need to reduce their susceptibility to negative peer influences by enhancing self-confidence and improving peer resistance skills, and they require careful monitoring of their behavior while at the same time providing them with increased personal responsibility.

Forming Intimate Relationships:
A Window of Opportunity

From early childhood, relationships with parents and family members have typically provided the closest feelings of connection to others and provide a base for resolving new developmental tasks and directions. Such close relationships are inherently constrained by kinships and norms, and thus they are not subject to choice or modification. From early adolescence until the establishment of dating relationships, however, teens look to their best friends to meet their needs for intimacy, companionship, nurturance, and assistance (Lempers & Clark-Lempers, 1992).

Early adolescence is a critical period for the development of close relationships, in which expectations regarding desirable characteristics in a friend are formed and guide the friendship selection process. Intimacy with peers is expressed initially through same-sex relationships in which youths share their private thoughts and feelings. At this stage they expect loyalty, commitment, and understanding from close friends, and expect to share their activities and interests with these friends (Clark & Ayers, 1993). Moreover, important gender differences emerge, in which females (as a group) expect more from their close relationships and report them to have more intimacy and self-disclosure than do males (Buhrmester & Furman, 1987). Such peer relationships are voluntary and more fluid than family and kinships, and are therefore formed and transformed with greater frequency (Laursen & Collins, 1994).

By midadolescence or so, romantic partners increase in their importance as social support providers (Furman & Buhrmester, 1985, 1992). The average length of partnerships increases gradually from 4 months for 15-year-olds to 9 months by age 18 (Feiring, 1995). For both genders, when considering long-term relationships of a year or more, teens indicate that reciprocity, commitment, and love are the most important relationship qualities they seek. In addition, initial patterns of conflict resolution begin to emerge. Girls are likely to show increasing emphasis on compromise with friends, rather than submission. Boys, on the other hand, rely almost exclusively on submission to resolve dispute with friends (Laursen & Collins, 1994).

What are the bases for healthy adolescent relationships and nonviolent conflict resolution? Simply stated, adolescents who have had close relationships with parents and friends in the past are more likely to have a strong base from which to develop future relationships and to resolve disagreements without resorting to violence or the abuse of power. Without such a foundation based on previous experiences and role models, a young person is more vulnerable to the powerful influences provided by the media, peers, and his or her own emotional disregulation. The methods they choose to resolve conflict, moreover, will shape the future outcomes of that relationship and many to come. Disagreements make a relationship better as often as they have no effect, especially among friends and romantic partners, and conflicts that involve constructive engagement seem to stimulate positive adaptation. For example, compromise and, to a lesser extent, disengagement serve to promote continual social interaction, whereas submission does not (Laursen & Collins, 1994).

How can these important changes in biological, cognitive, and interpersonal development be geared to the advantage of violence prevention efforts? In other health-related areas, such as sexual activity, weight control, smoking, and exercise, considerable progress has been made by capitalizing on the natural interest and motivation of youth to learn about lifestyle issues (Millstein, Petersen, & Nightingale, 1993). Greater self-understanding can be fostered through interventions in which teens learn to express personal points of view while keeping an open mind to alternative perspectives. Active exploration of alternative roles can be supported by community-based projects, apprenticeships, and other learning experiences. Youths may also build self-esteem by experiencing opportunities to feel competent and behave successfully. Self-efficacy and potency are bolstered by improving their life skills and providing the opportunity for community service. Support from peers, furthermore, can be increased by interventions or educational opportunities aimed at these social cognitive behavioral skills.

A Paradigm for
Youth Empowerment

> **BOX 4.2**
> "No major disorder affecting humankind has ever been brought under control or eliminated by attempts at treating the afflicted individual nor training large numbers of therapists" (John Gordon, quoted in Albee, 1985, p. 216).

Violence is often glamorized in the adolescent's world through popular television shows and musical groups that present violence as a commonplace and acceptable means of dealing with problems. The bombardment of exposure to violent, coercive, and sexist models of relationships (with ample forms of vicarious reinforcement) is coupled with the pressure often placed on youth to conform to gender-specific roles as they are seeking to form their own intimate and dating relationships. Regrettably, as youth begin to form important personal relationships, many are poorly informed about how to handle conflict and abuse.

Yet, adolescence also encompasses important learning opportunities and successful accomplishments that far outweigh the discriminatory view of youth as being antisocial or violent. For these reasons, we seek ways to work *with* youth to assist them in forming choices and in learning nonviolent means of communicating with their current and future partners. The transitional nature and normal disequilibrium that accompany adolescent development may represent an especially sensitive and opportune time for early intervention and enhancement experiences. From a societal perspective, an increasing demand for more long-lasting solutions is being echoed by more and more policymakers, professionals, and community groups as they become disillusioned with punitive strategies for dealing with youth crime and other forms of adolescent deviance (Millstein et al., 1993).

It is important to recognize as well that the adult world sometimes seems inconsistent and arbitrary to the adolescent, who may be faced with choices or options that do not reflect his or her perceived level of responsibility and self-guidance. These restrictions may be necessary for their (or our) safety, or seem reasonable from a developmental point of view, yet any "forbidden" activities then become attractive symbols of adult status. For example, society restricts teens' access to positively valued adult roles (e.g., full-time worker) and attempts to limit their involvement in valued adult behavior (such as sex and drinking). At the same time, we often assume that they are "old enough" to look after their own health, diet, education, and similar personal goals. These opposing expectations may, in turn, increase the functional value of some health-compromising behaviors—a youth may seek out opportunities to engage in forbidden activities simply because they send his or her parents a "message" of dissatisfaction (Millstein et al., 1993). Forming an identity of one's own, an important developmental milestone, can therefore be compromised by the lack of clear expectations, information, and guidance.

An important step toward bridging the immense gap between *restricted opportunities* and *self-guidance* for youth is the endorsement of an underlying philosophy that promotes inclusion and involvement of youth in their own issues and choices—responsibility rather than control; ownership rather than exclusion; empowerment rather than isolation. Prevention and promotion efforts are well-suited to this philosophy, whereas treatment and rehabilitation efforts, by their very definition, are poorly suited.

True prevention efforts are organized according to specified principles that are central to their purpose, as opposed to reactions to presenting problems or urgent needs. Establishing a set of principles for designing an intervention or educational effort requires a degree of recognition and understanding of purpose that often transcends the immediate demands of the situation or population; in other words, this process relies to a large extent on adequate vision, knowledge, and planning required to entrust individuals with the skills and responsibilities they may require.

A growing, yet still minority, perspective on youth places less emphasis on their wrongdoings and takes more interest in how youth serve as resources to their families, schools, and communities. Benard, Fafoglia, and McDonald (1991) argue for a paradigm shift that views youth not as problems to be fixed, but instead as resources to their families, schools, and communities. Youth must be supported with the information and skills needed to be actively involved in working toward prosocial change in the youth subculture and in their broader environment. Closeness with others develops by increasing interdependence and allowing individuals to become more invested in defining and choosing their own rewards. Moreover, asking youths directly about their own interests and goals, and listening to their replies, supports the underlying philosophy that their beliefs and attitudes are inherently important and worthy of consideration.

Recent evaluations of cooperative learning programs and those programs that place peers in teaching positions indicate increases in social interaction, peer acceptance, and greater acceptance of physically handicapped peers, mentally handicapped peers, or both following such learning opportunities (e.g., Maheady, Sacca, & Harper, 1988; Mesch, Lew, Johnson, & Johnson, 1986; Sisson, VanHasselt, Hersen, & Strain, 1985) and between white and non-white peers (Rooney-Rebeck & Jason, 1986; Slavin & Oickle, 1981). To this end we have defined several important principles in relation to the Youth Relationships Project: trust and respect, choice and voice, and respect and recognition. From this guiding philosophy we arrive at the principle of empowerment, a powerful agent to carry out our goals and objectives.

Trust and Responsibility

The foundation to an effective prevention endeavor is that each person is worthy of trust and should be given the chance (or many chances) to act responsibly. Because we are speaking of prevention of abuse and violence, rather than intervention, there is the explicit assumption that no preexisting breach of trust, infraction of the law or rules, or similar wrongdoing has occurred to belie this trust. Therefore, an individual can be accepted into a program on the basis of his or her interest and commitment, rather than as a requirement or alternative to treatment or punishment. A belief in the trustworthiness of the individual and his or her capability to act responsibility is important to empower individuals to make their own decisions. Without faith in oneself, an individual is limited in his or her ability and desire to make positive changes.

This principle is especially important for prevention efforts with teens, because they may take particular joy in "beating the system" (this motive is not surprising considering that the "system" offers few choices for this age group). By enacting the principle of trust and responsibility, teens are given an opportunity to develop responsibility and demonstrate trustworthiness, which further empowers them to make important decisions and follow through with appropriate actions.

The program, Teens as Community Resources (Langstaff, 1991), provides a good example of this philosophy. This program strives to empower young people to become active, problem-solving members of their communities by giving them small grants to develop community projects and youth organizations. Although teens are offered technical assistance from project staff (several of whom are teens), the responsibility lies with each individual to make their program work.

Choice and Voice

Another principle underlying prevention efforts is the need to give individuals a voice in the program, and a choice about what will be offered and how the information is delivered. By involving individuals from the beginning we are not only empowering them to take responsibility and think through important decisions, we are also developing their investment in prevention and problem resolution. Rather than relying on outside help once a problem has emerged or becomes critical, this principle describes the process whereby youths help to organize the very services they are to receive. Moreover, changes and additions to the materials can be based on "consumer demand," thus avoiding a hierarchy or conflict of goals and objectives that may be at odds (e.g., the service providers' goals and the recipients' goals).

The importance of this principle is illustrated by the comments made by youths who recently completed the full course of our Youth Relationship Project (YRP), designed to involve them in ways to promote healthy, nonviolent relationships. In response to the question "what did you like best or find most useful in the program" sample responses were the following:

> "The group worked together talking about a problem;"
> "Everyone talked openly, everyone put in their own comments;"
> "Talking to others and realizing that some people feel the same."

Respect and Recognition

Prevention efforts guided by principles also adhere to the respect and recognition of ethnic, cultural, racial, and sexual orientation differences. One of the most common themes reflected in comments about the YRP was that of respect—youths felt that their opinions and comments were never ridiculed, but rather were heard and considered. The following are examples:

"People were supportive of your opinion and you weren't laughed at;"
"It seemed like we were all equal, even the leaders;"
"No one was being judged by others, no hidden expectations."

For prevention efforts to be successful, it is necessary that those involved maintain an atmosphere in which individuals are recognized and respected as distinct, contributing members of the group. It is also necessary to acknowledge the unique challenges and perspectives of individuals in the group who may have different experiences, ethnic identification, sexual orientation, and similar characteristics than the majority. Minority youth tend to belong to groups that are relatively disadvantaged in terms of socioeconomical and educational opportunities and outcomes, and they face the challenge of navigating two different and often conflicting sets of cultural norms, values, and demands. Minority youth, as well as bisexual, gay, or lesbian youth, are more often the targets of prejudice, stereotyping, and discrimination. To respond to this injustice, curricula and activities should incorporate program aspects that address the needs of these often oppressed groups.

A good example of such specialized programming is illustrated in the Prevention of Black-on-Black Violence Program (Whaley, 1992). This prevention program incorporates language and values based on African American subculture, and examines issues and provides role models that are most salient to these youth. Through mutual recognition of racial and ethnic differences, teens begin to establish the necessary precursors for mutual respect and understanding.

BOX 4.3
Prevention of Black-on-Black Violence

This prevention program was specifically designed for African American youth, and it addresses the problem of violence in the their community. The program is organized into the following four units:

Unit 1: "Who kills black people?" is designed to dispel myths and stereotypes about black homicide, and to give factual information about black violence.

Unit 2: "Are blacks more violent than whites?" looks at racial stereotypes and gives black perspectives on violence—for example, those of Martin Luther King Jr., Malcolm X, and Nelson Mandela.

Unit 3: "When is the time to fight?" explores reasons for interpersonal violence and looks at violence on a personal level.

Unit 4: "Knowing when to chill" deals with coping techniques, such as stress-inoculation training and relaxation techniques.

Empowerment

The previous principles lead us directly to the discussion of empowerment. Much of the recent work related to empowerment is based on feminist theory, which explores the meaning of the permanent inequality in relationships in which one member is defined as unequal by society on the basis of their sex, race, class, or other characteristics ascribed by birth (Miller, 1986). Empowerment has a special attraction to working with youth, especially in conjunction with our particular emphasis on the importance of *relationships* as key methods of learning and developing interpersonal skills. Empowerment, furthermore, reflects the active manner in which we put our principles into practice, and the concept incorporates many of the implicit as well as explicit principles underlying prevention and health promotion.

The juxtaposition of the concepts of "powerlessness" and "empowerment" merit attention. Both concepts have grown in appeal in recent years, perhaps because they reflect the sociopolitical influences on health and behavior as well as the reciprocal nature of risk and protective factors (i.e., the environment acts on the individual, and the individual acts on the environment). Powerlessness refers to an individual's (or family's, community's, and so on) sense of alienation, victim blaming, and learned helplessness in relation to their ability to effect change or direct their lives (Wallerstein, 1992).

Not surprisingly, this phenomenon incorporates many of the physical and social risk factors that are connected to a feeling of lack of control over one's destiny, which in turn leads to an increased likelihood of poor physical or mental health. Thus, powerless individuals feel despair at their ability to effect any change or have any control over their experiences, because they experience greater oppression, lack of choice, and limited freedom, and often lack connections to an increasingly complex social system (Wallerstein, 1992).

It is not difficult to conclude that, in general, youths objectively lack power in the political and economic system. Rather than viewing youths as a valued and significant part of society, there appears to be a mismatch between their needs and abilities and the opportunities afforded to them. Similarly, although each individual may possess a high degree of personal power or self-efficacy, collectively young adults are limited in their choices and connections to the larger adult world. Unfortunately, for some this lack of power can collide with the dominant North American ideology of equality of opportunity, thereby forcing them to consider why they are unsuccessful at achieving these societal promises. A common response to such failure or frustration is to blame oneself or to blame particular aspects of society (such as schools, police, political figures) for what is, in reality, a systemwide discrimination.

Empowerment, on the other hand, refers to the manner in which people assume control and mastery over their lives, especially within the context of their social and political reality. Wallerstein (1992) provides a clear definition of empowerment in relation to both the individual and the broader social structure:

In its broadest definition, empowerment is a multilevel construct that involves people assuming control and mastery over their lives in the context of their social and political environment; they gain a sense of control and purposefulness to exert political power as they participate in the democratic life of their community for social change. It is an ecological construct that applies to interactive change on multiple levels: the individual, organization, and community. A study of empowerment, therefore, implies not just studying individual change, but also change in the social setting itself . . . it is a social action process that promotes participation of people, organizations, and communities toward the goals of increased individual and community control, political efficacy, improved quality of community life, and social justice. (p. 198)

Thus, a lack of control over destiny promotes a susceptibility to ill health for people who are marginalized. Empowerment counters this process by challenging social and physical risk factors in a setting in which people can gain belief in their ability to control their own worlds and work together. In the following figure, Figure 4.1, Wallerstein (1992) provides a very useful summary of the social and physical risk factors that may lead to either a sense of powerlessness or empowerment.

Several important principles are contained within an empowerment model: *fairness*, or the concept of equity and justice; *integrity and honesty*, which provides a foundation of trust; *human dignity*, which acknowledges worth and value; *service*, which encourages and teaches individuals how they can make a contribution; and *potential and growth*, which recognizes an individual's ability to grow at his or her own pace, and that potential for further growth (rather than outcome or destination alone) is worth pursuing. An *empowerment model*, therefore, is one that helps an individual to perceive himself or herself as a "causal agent" in achieving solutions to salient issues and to perceive the service provider as having knowledge and skills that are of personal value and interest.

A look at how an empowerment model may be applied to the needs and interests of adolescents requires further consideration of the processes of change. First, empowerment entails an integrated approach that recognizes that merely providing information and teaching skills is not sufficient for healthy development. Recipients must have or develop the motivation to use information, skills, and

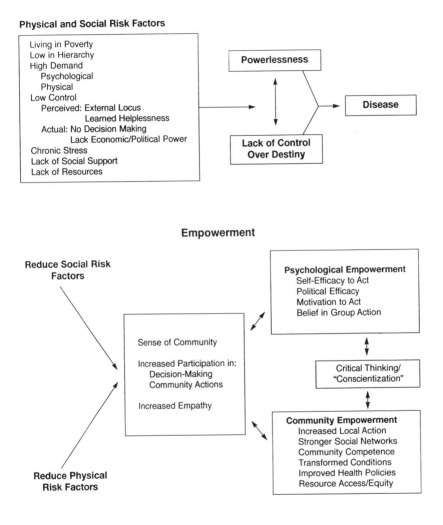

Figure 4.1. Summary of the Social and Physical Risk Factors That May Lead to Either a Sense of Powerlessness or Empowerment

SOURCE: Wallerstein, N. (1992). Powerlessness, empowerment, and health: Implications for health promotion programs. *American Journal of Health Promotion, 6,* 197-205. Reprinted with permission.

services on their own behalf. Second, evidence suggests that one's sense of personal power is further enhanced by a "sense of community." A feeling of belongingness and connection to similar others greatly enhances one's commitment and interest, which is the key for developing *group power* (Chavis & Wandersman, 1990). For adolescents, for example, networks of family members, peers, and caring adults are a valued component to youth empowerment. This sets up a reciprocal process, or interaction, in which decision making and community actions enhance psychological empowerment and these empowered individuals, in turn, become more likely to participate in community action.

An Empowerment Education Model is described by Wallerstein (1992), based on the seminal work of Brazilian educator Paulo Freire (cited in Wallerstein, 1992). To actualize the important facets of empowerment noted previously, education must essentially engage people (through a dialogue process) in identifying their problems; critically assess the social, historical, and cultural roots of their problems; and develop action strategies to change their personal and social lives. The participatory, social orientation to teaching empowerment strategies involves three sequential steps:

1. Listening and making the participants feel they are "co-investigators" of their shared problems. According to Wallerstein, this process uncovers issues of emotional and social significance, and becomes the basis for strategies to effect change.
2. Developing a "dialogue" about those issues that were uncovered during the listening phase. Each person (including the "teacher") participates as an equal to consider the problems raised, to explore the roots of those problems, and to consider alternatives (i.e., a process of critical thinking).
3. Following this process of critical thinking, participants need to move beyond what they perceive as the causes of their problems to become more involved in the solutions (i.e., personal and social actions). Personal involvement unites people as members of a common community, and provides a greater impetus toward transforming inequities into strengths.

Finally, it is necessary to recognize that translating empowerment from theory into practice requires careful consideration of program development and delivery. Goals must be examined to ensure they do not foster dependence and that they enable participants to assume responsibility for their own program and curriculum. Curricula, moreover, should provide ample opportunity for people to build trust and to share their own issues and concerns in a safe and helpful environment.

The active agent in empowerment is participation, and a cooperative peer model encourages youth to support one another while providing a venue to model positive attitudes and values. The essential qualities of healthy relationships are developed in which youth have the opportunity to work together toward common goals in a respectful, supportive group setting (Benard et al., 1991).

CHAPTER FIVE

A Developmental Model of Relationship Violence and Abuse

For the majority, adolescence is a period of healthy growth. Physical, cognitive, and psychosocial maturity come together as the adolescent moves toward adult life. For some vulnerable youths, however, this period of development is marked by conflict and uncertainty as they attempt to form intimate relationships with peers and dating partners in the absence of healthy role models. Additionally, because of their own familiarity with violence and abuse during their earlier development, these vulnerable youths may have particular difficulty recognizing their own abusive behavior or their options to terminate an abusive relationship.

It is these vulnerable youth, who share a preponderance of risk factors and lack appropriate protective mechanisms, to whom we place our emphasis. An increased risk of relationship violence can be anticipated for these individuals, because the foundations for such violence are *organized* in childhood but are often *activated* in adolescence (Earls, Cairns, & Mercy, 1993).

In this chapter we use the analogy of a "funnel of violence," in which known risk factors from cultural, familial, peer, and individual sources become more and more potent for selected individuals who are unable to escape being drawn toward the opening. These risk factors associated with violence in peerships and partnerships may also cluster with other adolescent risk behaviors due to common etiology (Millstein & Igra, 1995). For example, teens who experienced child maltreatment are also more likely to become pregnant in adolescence (Gershenson et al., 1989) and to become an early substance abuser (for females), and a user of a greater variety of drugs (for males; Harrison, Hoffmann, & Edwall, 1989a, 1989b). Importantly, the following model provides a conceptual basis for considering how such risk factors may be deactivated prior to or during adolescence.

The Funnel of Violence: General to Specific Risk Factors

Violence risk factors refer to those events or characteristics that increase the likelihood of a child developing interpersonal violence compared to those children who do not have such events or characteristics with which to contend. We conceptualize these risk factors as moving from the general to the more specific, that is, general risk factors are operative for all youth, whereas specific risk factors are primarily operative for youths who are at greatest risk for relationship violence (i.e., "vulnerable" youth). From this perspective, general risk factors may make violence more likely because they are associated with, but not directly responsible for, violent outcomes.

For example, although low socioeconomic status is often associated with harsh parental practices and child abuse, socioeconomic status in and of itself does not account for interpersonal violence (e.g., Davis & Allen, 1995). More specific risk factors, on the other hand, are those causal agents that are most directly linked to increased likelihood of violent outcomes, such as deviant peer groups, harsh family disciplinary practices, and certain personality characteristics.

Figure 5.1 depicts a hypothetical "funnel of violence." At the mouth of the funnel are experiences that most youth are exposed to on a regular basis—the blatant as well as subtle societal and cultural messages that glorify, glamorize, or exploit violent and abusive behavior. These include the prevailing culture, with its stereotypical view of the sexes and related legal and social policies, including its tolerance of relationship violence. It also includes the youth subculture, those exalted heroes and their heroic acts, rock stars, sport figures, celebrities, and the things they do (and get away with). The "messengers" of societal and cultural influences include the media, neighborhoods and communities, and social policies. From an intervention perspective, it remains an open question as to whether we should "shoot the messengers," (i.e., poising our intervention at the institutions), or whether we should simply target or counteract the nature of their messages.

As we move toward the more narrow opening of the funnel we approach those agents within our families who serve as the "filters" for the broader proviolent messages of our culture. Living in a violent or abusive home, which includes the wide range of physical and emotional acts that define violence, constitutes an important "training" experience both in ways of being abusive toward others and in ways of survival and coping. In the family, exposure to relationship violence (either as a victim or an offender) may come to establish the youth's primary frame of reference as being one of control and power.

These experiences translate into a significant dilemma for the adolescent who is in the process of forming his or her own intimate relationships; personal experiences of violence and abuse create a central relationship theme and conflict resolution strategy ("if it works, use it"). Furthermore, if someone suggests to the youth that there are effective alternatives to violence or that their behavior is inappropriate, the youth has little else to go by ("sounds nice, but it's not for me"). These familial influences lay the foundation for two important lessons in the creation of interpersonal violence: learning to abuse power and learning to fear others.

These cognitive, emotional, and behavioral learning experiences within the family directly influence the youth's social network, the peers and partners with whom the youth connects. Again, it is the

FUNNEL OF VIOLENCE

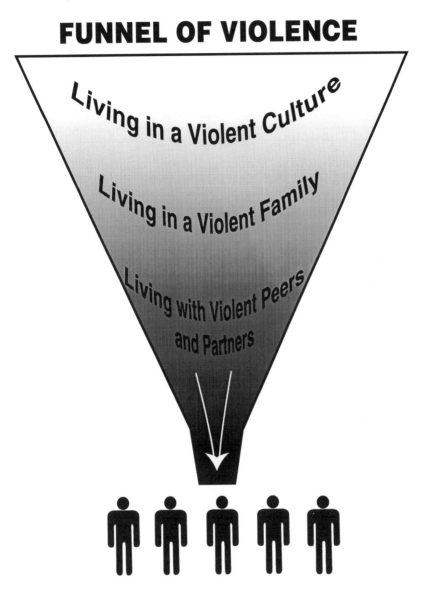

Figure 5.1. The Funnel of Violence: The Flow From General to More Specific Risk Factors That Increase One's Vulnerability to Violence in Relationships

nature of the connection that promotes and facilitates relationship violence. At-risk youth tend to "hook up" with, and therefore be reinforced by, similar at-risk youth (Dodge, Pettit, & Bates, 1994).

Finally, as we approach the most narrow end of the funnel we consider the psychological characteristics of at-risk youths themselves. Their individual limitations or challenges (such as aggression, impulsivity, and self-esteem problems) may interact with these prevailing environmental influences in a dynamic and compelling way that winds up leading to violent relationships, antisocial activity, or both.

The funnel of violence describes relationship risk factors for the adolescent that range from more general to specific, with each layer "building on" the strength of the next. This "nested" model is derived from Bronfenbrenner's (1979) ecological paradigm, in which contextual factors function at increasing distances from the "target" child (i.e., moving outward from the child, from proximal to distal influences). Rather than postulate that each system only has varying degrees of effect on the child, Bronfenbrenner included interactions among systems in the immediate environment as a separate domain of study (for instance, how parents interact with the school system).

Thus, at the heart of interacting environmental systems are people from different environments interacting with each other, in more or less adaptive ways for the child. Interpersonal relationships, therefore, that are contained within the various layers of peer, family, school, and cultural influences are crucial to understanding the risk of violence during adolescence. From adult-to-child, adult-to-youth, child-to-child, and youth-to-youth, it is the relationship that provides the emotional valence to these various sources of socialization.

Figure 5.2 depicts our proposed developmental model of interpersonal violence, which attempts to capture the various background or "setting events" for relationship dysfunction among youth. These contexts are considered to function at two levels: a *general level* that denotes a risk factor for the entire population of youth (i.e., it affects about everyone), and a *specific level* that denotes a risk for vulnerable youth (i.e., it affects some more than others). Put another way, we are attempting to capture the complexity of violence in relation-

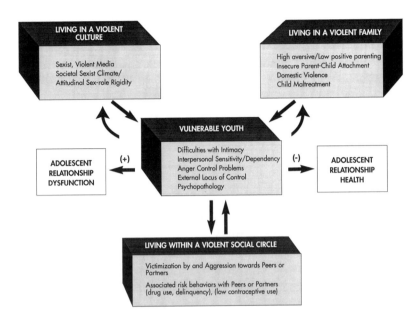

Figure 5.2. A Developmental Model of Interpersonal Violence

ships, while understanding that some youths (by virtue of their individual differences in personality or other stable characteristics) will be more influenced by various familial and cultural experiences than other, perhaps more resilient, youths.

For example, if we consider the five dimensions shown in Figure 5.2 under the heading Vulnerable Youth (i.e., difficulties with intimacy, interpersonal sensitivity/dependency, anger control problems, external locus of control, and psychopathology) we form the picture of young persons who have more difficulties in modulating their emotions and arousal, in how they present themselves and approach others (i.e., less easy to get along with), in their tendency to attribute problems to causes outside of themselves (yet attribute successes to themselves), and who have more psychological difficulties with which to contend. Not all vulnerable youths are expected to display all of these features, although some may; rather, each vulnerable youth is assumed to possess at least one of these challenging individual characteristics. This conceptualization is not exhaustive and some very important individual differences (for example, intelligence, cognitive "tempo," organizational and problem-solving skills) would also be likely to play a role in individual vulnerability.

Thus, a vulnerable youth would be at a greater disadvantage when experiencing the general negative familial and cultural variables shown in Figure 5.2. In turn, these disadvantages may play a contributing role to the individual's further experiences of *violence-specific* familial and cultural variables. For instance, although child maltreatment is always an adult action and adult responsibility, abusive adults are sometimes selective in the severity of abuse they direct toward specific children (Wekerle & Wolfe, 1996). A similar analogy is made to the effect of viewing television violence on aggression in children, with the argument being that children inclined toward aggression are "attracted" to aggressive television programs and have a more elaborated frame of reference within which to process such aggressive information (Eron, 1982). Thus, we would expect the vulnerable youth to have an elevated level of experiencing childhood trauma (such as physical or sexual abuse, witnessing parental violence, and so on) as well as greater exposure and "connection" to violent, sexist cultural messages and experiences.

Essentially, we are proposing that being a vulnerable youth and experiencing violence-specific familial and cultural contexts is a potent combination for adolescent relationship dysfunction (in general). Violence-specific indicators of relationship dysfunction, which we have labeled the victim/victimizer view of relationships, adversarial relationships beliefs, and negative affectivity in relationships, then play a major role in accentuating the risk of interpersonal violence. In other words, a youth who shows an elevated personal risk has not only a less flexible view and approach to forming bonds with others, but the nature of these bonds harken back to the childhood trauma they endured, in which there were two very salient and clearly defined roles to any dyad—the victim and the victimizer. Also, in a related manner, relationships have come to acquire a particular aversive hue, with expectations of harm, injury, abandonment, and hurt. Even when things would seem to be going well or just O.K., such a youth feels a certain uneasiness in relationships, waiting out the calm before the storm, because things simply seem and feel "too good to be true."

In tying this together, our developmental model of adolescent interpersonal violence suggests that disadvantaged children, raised in disadvantaged settings with few positive influences to provide an alternative frame of reference, are most likely to carry the violence in their lives forward to their intimate partnerships, either as a victim of violence, a perpetrator of violence, or both. This developmental pathway is indicated by the plus (+) sign shown on the path from "vulnerable youth" to "adolescent relationship dysfunction" in Figure 5.2, to symbolize the positive association (or "loading") between these factors. Similarly, the minus (-) sign on the path from "vulnerable youth" to "adolescent relationship health" depicts the inverse relationship between these risk factors and positive relationship outcomes. All of the negative influences that have increased the likelihood of relationship dysfunction also severely limit the youth's chances of having positive, nonviolent, egalitarian, supportive relationships.

We now consider these major components in turn, with a special focus on how they influence (singly and in combination) the nature and expression of the adolescent's relationship development.

The Cultural Context: Normative Expectations

Modern culture has strong undercurrents of violence as expressed through racism, sexism, classism, and similar oppression (Miedzian, 1995). Despite their theoretical and clinical appeal, however, these cultural and societal factors have not undergone the level of study required to make strong research-based claims of direct effects. Clearly, millions of children each day are exposed to media conveying the value, acceptability, and even normalcy of violence in relationships as well as specific themes of interpersonal aggression, male dominance, and female invisibility and subordination. This layer of negative influence is supported by studies showing a fairly prevalent attitudinal acceptance of intimate violence. For example, 20% of male high school students endorsed forced intercourse under certain circumstances (e.g., "if they had been dating for a long time," "if he spent money on her"; Sudermann & Jaffe, 1993) and 80% of female college students endorsed physical force, with 18% identifying situations of "playing" and the male being "out of control" (Roscoe, 1985).

Fortunately, it seems similarly apparent that even though many children and youth are exposed to sexism, violence, and other forms of oppression in their daily doses of cultural entertainment, most will not go on to become violent toward an intimate partner. Such resilient individuals inform us of many of the creative as well as fortuitous ways that relationship violence can be avoided and risk factors overcome. Those youth who are most vulnerable, however, due to their family experiences and personal resources in particular, also appear to be the ones who are most attracted to and influenced by the broader cultural messages depicting "in" and "out" groups, rigid power structures and destructive myths (i.e., "might is right"; victims get their "just deserts").

In the following sections we discuss two of the more influential societal and cultural forces that seem to play most directly to vulnerable youth: sex-role rigidity, and sexist, violent media.

Gender Roles and Gender Rigidity

A feminist perspective on domestic violence focuses on the process of sex-role socialization as central to men's violence against their female partners (e.g., Dobash & Dobash, 1992; Miedzian, 1995). Power inequality between the genders and active devaluation of females is considered one of the fundamental supports to violence against women (Sudermann, Jaffe, & Hastings, 1995). Gender-role rigidity is viewed as a product of "traditional" socialization practices, in which boys are raised to be strong, uncommunicative, competitive, and in control, and girls are raised to be compliant, other-oriented, and not to express anger directly (Serbin, Powlishta, & Gulko, 1993).

Restriction of gender roles is believed to reinforce negative attitudes and power imbalances in male/female relationships (Dobash

& Dobash, 1992). Similarly, gender-based, inflexible attitudes about each partner's role in a relationship often translate into the belief that the woman is responsible for the relationship, including the happiness and well-being of her male partner, and the man is entitled to greater focus within a relationship. In a complementary process, gender-role rigidity may also translate into a man's tendency toward compartmentalizing female partners according to the separate functions they can perform for him (e.g., "Madonna" and "whore" view of women; Dutton, 1994).

There is empirical evidence that the behaviors of boys and girls are reinforced differently by parents, teachers, and peers. For example, males are attended to more often than girls, their aggression is more successful in resolving disputes than female verbal persuasion, and female negative emotion is attended to less often than male negative emotion (see Birns, Cascardi, & Meyer, 1994). Additionally, there is evidence that the mother-son and mother-daughter relationships differ in terms of when mothers exhibit sensitivity toward their child. Biringen, Robinson, and Emde (1994), for example, found that more sensitive interactions between mothers and their sons generally occurred when the son led the flow of interactions, whereas the more sensitive interaction between mothers and daughters involved greater maternal control of the interactional flow. Additionally, mother-son interactions were marked by greater elaboration and mutual control. Although not the only factor by far, these data are consistent with the notion that boys are encouraged toward greater autonomy and given greater license to "control" the flow of interactions, whereas girls are encouraged toward greater compliance with authority and given less license to directly influence others.

Pleck, Sonenstein, and Ku (1993) provide compelling evidence of the importance of traditional attitudes toward masculinity and their role in shaping intimate relationships. Based on an analysis of the 1988 U.S. National Survey of Adolescent Males, these researchers found that boys who held traditional attitudes toward masculinity (termed "masculine ideology") generally behaved in a gender-based, stereotypical fashion toward young women. For example, they reported having more sexual partners in the past year, with a less intimate relationship at the time of their last intercourse with their partner. In addition, they held greater beliefs that relationships between men and women are adversarial, held more negative attitudes toward condom use, showed less current use of condoms, held less belief in males' responsibility to prevent pregnancy, and held a greater belief that pregnancy validates their masculinity. On the basis of their findings, the researchers conclude that traditional masculine ideology is associated with characteristics that may limit the quality of adolescent males' close heterosexual relationships, thus increasing the risk of sexually related diseases.

The direct link between sex-role rigidity and relationship violence has received only limited empirical study to date, however. For example, Stith and Farley (1993) found that low levels of sex-role egalitarianism (tolerance of nontraditional sex roles) predicted both an attitudinal approval of marital violence and reports of marital violence. Because these results were found for a group of adult males attending support groups for battering and alcoholism, their applicability to at-risk adolescents remains unclear. Our research team studied attitudes and beliefs about relationship violence in a community sample of high school students, and found that youths reporting greater childhood maltreatment also reported more hostility toward others, as well as more proviolent attitudes toward partners (e.g., endorsing the use of power-assertive methods with romantic partners) than youths reporting no to low levels of childhood maltreatment (Wolfe, Wekerle, Reitzel-Jaffe, & Lefebvre, 1995). Taken together, these data suggest that stereotypical views of male and female roles characterize the "mind set" of youth at risk for relationship violence, which also seems to be associated with increased youth risk behaviors (see Peers and Partners section that follows).

Sexist and Violent Media

The Entertainment Value of Violence and Abuse

It is common knowledge that violence is often glamorized in the adolescent's world, with popular television shows, advertisements, and musical groups presenting violence as a commonplace and acceptable means of dealing with problems. The bombardment of exposure to violent, coercive, and sexist models of relationships (with ample forms of vicarious reinforcement) is coupled with the pressure often put on youths to conform to gender-specific roles as they are seeking to form their own intimate and dating relationships. The media helps this process of confusion along, for example, through attractive portrayals of sex and substance use in television programs and ads. Regrettably, as youth begin to form important personal relationships, many are poorly informed as to how to handle such arousal and competing interests. Such media are not solely responsible for antisocial behavior and gender-based violence, yet they are considered important background influences (Murray, J. P., 1995).

Television and Movies. A look at what many of our children do with their time provides a useful introduction to the ways that violence is socialized into the lives of children and youth. Almost all North American households have at least one TV set. According to the American Psychological Association task force report on television and American society (Huston et al., 1992), by the time the average child (that is, a child who watches 2 to 4 hours of television each day) finishes elementary school, he or she will have witnessed at least 8,000 murders and more than 100,000 other acts of violence on television.

Given these numbers, it is not surprising that research over the past three decades has found significant negative effects from viewing TV violence on children's beliefs, knowledge, attitudes and, ultimately, their behavior (e.g., Comstock & Paik, 1994; Eron, Huesmann, Lefkowitz, & Walder, 1972; Huston et al., 1992; Signorielli, 1991). In fact, psychological research has led to three prominent effects of seeing violence on television (National Association for the Education of Young Children, 1990):

Children may become less sensitive to the pain and suffering of others;
Children may be more fearful of the world around them;
Children may be more likely to behave in aggressive or harmful ways toward others.

It is understandable how children and youth may obtain the idea that violence/abuse is acceptable (or at least normative) among intimate relationships, when they observe the following on TV (based on a substantive review by Malamuth & Briere, 1986):

- In the vast majority of portrayals of sexual violence, men are the aggressors and women are the victims.
- Sexual violence continues to increase (but remains less common than the portrayal of nonsexual violence).
- Sexual aggression is often depicted quite differently from nonsexual aggression, in that suffering or trauma is often expected of the female victims of sexual violence.

In addition, Comstock & Paik (1994) summarize some of the principle ways in which violence portrayed on television and in movies may heighten the potential influence on children:

- Reward or lack of punishment or consequences for the perpetrators of violence;
- Portrayal of violence as being justified in some way, due to circumstances;
- Portrayal of the perpetrator of violence as someone who is similar to the viewer;
- Portrayal of violence as real events, rather than concocted;
- Portrayal of violent acts that please the viewer.

In short, television and similar audio-visual media are representative of the manner in which children and youth may be absorbing important messages concerning interpersonal relationships (Huston et al., 1992). Regardless of the possible direct effects of viewing violence on television, greater sensitivity is needed in the way in which messages are being provided to children and youth, and how these messages may be distorted in the minds of some individuals to facilitate adversarial beliefs and hostile attitudes toward others.

The social, political, and economic progress made by women over the past 50 years is also reflected in an uneven and distorted manner by the media. A Canadian Radio-Television and Telecommunications Commission (CRTC, 1990) study found that men and women are still depicted differently in almost every area of broadcasting, from programming to advertising, on both radio and television. In television drama, significantly more women are married, interact with children, participate in home management, and have a supervisor at work, whereas significantly more men have paid employment, are in status positions, operate vehicles, and commit acts of physical violence (CRTC, 1990).

Even more disturbing is the portrayal of sex roles in films. Female actors are stereotypically presented as relatively powerless and passive whereas males are presented as relatively bad, which generates similar sentiments in the individual viewer (Hedley, 1994). These cultural presentations, based on many years of repeated imagery, form a major part of the base of some men's motivation to maintain control and power in a relationship: Women are encouraged to defer to the benevolence of powerful men, and men are encouraged to challenge the autonomy of powerful and assertive women.

BOX 5.1

"Try to picture a female slasher monster who kills man after man after man. Now imagine that character making millions for an independent production company in eight sequels—each more gruesome than the last. Picture her image dominating video stores displays and home screens, and spawning hundreds of licensed products: dolls, greeting cards, masks, and plastic replicas of her favorite weapon. Then imagine all the little girls in the United States begging to costume themselves as that character for Halloween" (Maio, 1990, p. 42).

Stereotypic views of women as submissive and men as being dominant are reinforced by many of the media portrayals of violent and nonviolent acts. Moreover, violence is often modeled and fit into life experiences, so that it becomes commonplace and therefore normative. Not surprisingly, proaggressive attitudes and beliefs are modeled by the aggressors (and sometimes the victims themselves), again reinforcing one's belief that violence is acceptable under certain circumstances.

The principle concerns regarding television viewing and children's development were highlighted by a U.S. government task force (Milavsky, Kessler, Stipp, & Rubens, 1982). Based on two decades of research, the committee concluded that relatively powerless subgroups, such as children and institutionalized individuals, are especially vulnerable to the distorted roles and expectations depicted by television, because they sometimes lack the intellectual and social skills needed to evaluate and resist televised messages. Not surprisingly, they also concluded that the quantity of television viewing was not nearly as important as *what they watch*. For example, the volume of general media consumption has not been shown to correlate with sexual permissiveness, whereas exposure to sexually suggestive materials (such as Music Television and R-rated films), is significantly correlated with premarital sexual permissiveness among youth (Strouse, Buerkel-Rothfuss, & Long, 1995).

Music Videos. It is particularly noteworthy that both experimental and survey studies show a stronger connection between various attitudinal and behavioral indexes and exposure to music videos *than any other form of media expression*. Rock music has always reflected rebelliousness, and antisocial and sexually provocative images of young people (after all, it is their music). With the advent of rock music videos in 1981, however, the high-impact visual and auditory messages became a powerful marketing success, thus raising questions as to the possible negative influence of such videos. Of concern is the possibility of viewer's *desensitization to violence*, a phenomenon known to occur in other real-world scenarios in which exposure to violence becomes routine or commonplace (Averill, 1983). Additionally, viewing rock videos has been shown experimentally to have the same effect as viewing pornography: Male subjects express more calloused and antagonistic attitudes toward women (e.g., Peterson & Pfost, 1989).

Clearly, the distortion of gender roles and expectancies is intensified in music videos. According to a 1990 CRTC survey of English-language TV, the overall proportion of female characters in music videos is 30%, representing 3% of instrumental players, 19% of singers, and 40% of dancers. We should also be concerned about the way that women are typically portrayed in videos. In a report released by the Quebec Council on the Status of Women (Baby, Chéné, & Dudas, 1992), 55% of all rock videos were considered to be sexist (i.e., women were portrayed in submissive or sexually suggestive roles), an increase from 45% in 1988. These distorted portrayals of men and women help to form and reinforce societal stereotypes, and are influential in shaping the normative beliefs of young people about relationships, gender relations, and expectations.

Because such sexist or misogynous portrayals of male-female relationships are relatively common, there is additional concern that some young men will form beliefs that sexually aggressive behavior is sanctioned by society and is not deviant, especially when the victim is an acquaintance (Hall & Hirschman, 1991). Similarly, there is recent evidence that misogynous rap music, in which musical lyrics express the same negative and sexist attitudes as pornographic material (including the idea that sexual violence is enjoyable for women) facilitates sexually aggressive behavior among college-aged men (Barongan & Hall, 1995).

In closing, the question is once again raised concerning those conditions that might make some youth more susceptible to violent or sexist messages while others remain unaffected. Cultivation theory, which argues that TV helps shape viewers' perceptions of social reality, is most germane to an understanding of this process, although TV does not exert a one-way influence—a dynamic, ongoing process of interaction between the medium and the viewer seems to best fit the findings (Gerbner, Gross, Morgan, & Signorielli, 1986).

Using at-risk youths as an example, this theory implies that unsatisfactory conditions in a family promote the affective need for a young person to select and attend to music videos that enable escapism and fantasy. The video may seem more personal and intense than it might to another person from a more satisfactory family environment. For example, Strouse et al. (1995) found that girls from dissatisfactory family backgrounds were most vulnerable to the sexually permissive messages of these videos; not only did their attitudes change toward sexual permissiveness, but their endorsement of more permissive sexual behavior changed as well in relation to exposure. Such emotional vulnerability appears to make the minds of these young persons more receptive to the cultivating effect of viewing and listening. As a result, their perception of intimate relationships, sexual involvement, and romance begins to reflect those presented in the video.

The Family Context:
Early Models of Relationships

The pathways through which caregivers may influence an individual's expression of aggression and violence in relationships are complex. Although there is no clear evidence as to which factors are necessary and sufficient and how they may exert their influence over time, developmental theories propose that negative parent-child interactions lay the foundations for long-term problems forming relationships (Sroufe, 1989). Dix (1991), for example, notes the similarities in parenting styles among abusive, depressed, and distressed parents. Increased negative affect and the use of arbitrary, restrictive, and punitive strategies are common, with a concomitant decrease in positive affect or positive control strategies. Such a child-rearing environment is strongly linked to child antisocial behavior (Greenberg, Speltz, & DeKlyen, 1993; Vuchinich, Bank, & Patterson, 1992; Wahler & Dumas, 1986) and a greater preponderance of coercive relationships with peers and partners (e.g., Malamuth, Sockloskie, Koss, & Tanaka, 1991).

Children from abusive families have experienced more than just violence and victimization, they have also experienced an ambient family structure that fails to provide appropriate socialization opportunities to promote cooperative, "fair," healthy relationship styles. Additionally, such experiences further serve to disrupt and interfere with normal developmental processes, creating a "domino effect" on development (Wolfe & Jaffe, 1991). Critically, it is precisely the experience of maltreatment that may both accelerate and distort the transfer of interpersonal loyalties from caregivers to peers to ameliorate unmet needs in the home environment (Mueller & Silverman, 1989).

The Role of Early
Attachment and Maltreatment

Attachment theory provides an elaborate, lifespan explanation of the importance of relationships, through its emphasis on "internal working models" of relationships that form from a very early age. Attachment theory (Bowlby, 1969/1982, 1972, 1980) identifies that children form mental representations of themselves in relationships and of others as relationship partners, based on their history with significant caregivers (the primary caretaker in particular). These early models of relationships are thought to organize subsequent interactions with others, both in terms of the way in which a child responds to interactions and in the way a child actively shapes or sets in motion certain model-consistent interactional dynamics.

The two main types of models articulated by attachment theory are secure and insecure, with insecure being further differentiated into avoidant (exhibiting more behaviors signaling detachment) and anxious-ambivalent types (exhibiting more behaviors signaling protest, proximity seeking; Ainsworth, Blehar, Waters, & Wall, 1978). The secure child is confident in the availability of the attachment figure and, consequently, less likely to experience intense or chronic anxiety, fear, and anger about relationships and separation from attachment figures.

Although such models derived from early attachment experiences undergo transformations and elaborations throughout life, evidence points to a consistency in attachment models (Waters, Posada, Crowell, & Lay, 1993). Thus, this theory has important relevance to the formation of romantic partnerships and, ostensibly, the expectations, beliefs, and patterns underlying our treatment of others.

In pursuing this issue, Hazan and Shaver (1987) propose that adult romantic love is an attachment process, guided by the same relationship style tendencies evident in childhood (i.e., secure, avoidant, and anxious-ambivalent). In a series of related studies with college-aged subjects, these researchers found evidence for the three distinct attachment orientations (or "styles"). Notably, each style was associated with different beliefs about romantic love relationships—the availability and trustworthiness of love partners, and the love-worthiness of the individual. For instance, compared to insecure adults, secure individuals tended to describe their most important love experience as happy, friendly, and trusting; report longer duration of partnership; and tended to have a "realistic" view of partnerships as waxing and waning, with intermittent intense love periods. Insecure individuals, on the other hand, characterized their most important relationship as involving jealousy and emotional highs and lows. In particular, avoidant adults reported fears of intimacy and anxious-ambivalent adults reported love as involving obsession, desire for reciprocation and union, and extreme sexual attraction.

Furthermore, Hazan and Shaver (1987) found that these adult relationships bore important similarities to the way in which these individuals described their relationships with their parents. For instance, secure adults identified their parents as more respectful and accepting than did insecure adults. Although these findings were based on retrospective data, studies that have simultaneously assessed parents and adolescents have found a similar pattern of results. For example, Martin (1990) found that a style of avoidance and verbal aggression in the parent-teen relationship was consistent across the teen-partner relationship. For males, son-mother verbal aggression was significantly related to son-girlfriend verbal aggression. For females, interparental conflict predicted both mother-daughter and father-daughter verbal aggression, which in turn was predictive of daughter-boyfriend verbal aggression. Thus, there appears to be a trend toward using the same relationship styles with partners as experienced with caregivers.

Attachment theory provides an important conceptual framework for understanding relationship style (Hazan & Shaver, 1987, 1994) and violence in relationships in particular (Crittenden & Ainsworth, 1989). When violence exists in family systems, certain parameters may come to define a child's relational world. In maltreating families, violence and intimidation are given credence as viable strategies for maintaining relationships and resolving relationship conflicts (Cicchetti & Howes, 1991). The insecure, disorganized attachment of many maltreated children suggests that no single clear approach to relationships exist (Carlson, Cicchetti, Barnett, & Brunwald, 1989). Instead, the maltreated child must flexibly deploy proximity seeking, avoidance, and resistance toward the primary caregiver, as the winds of caregiver change would appear to dictate (Crittenden, 1988).

An inconsistent, insecure, and fearful context of the attachment relationship may thereby set the stage for future interactions to be characterized by approach-avoidance conflicts, in which the maltreated child may play out both victim and victimizer roles (Cicchetti & Howes, 1991; Crittenden & Ainsworth, 1989). In this manner, the maltreated child forms representational models of relationships that involve "victims and victimizers," with the maltreated child alternating between being the aggressor and the victim (Dodge et al., 1994). We have found additional support for this relationship between attachment models and subsequent relationship problems among a sample of 350 high-school students. Youths having significant maltreatment in their background differed from nonmaltreated youths in reporting greater levels of hostility toward others, and more physically and sexually coercive behavior toward their partners (Wolfe, Wekerle, Reitzel-Jaffe, & Lefebvre, 1995).

Generally speaking, therefore, insecure attachment models are associated with greater interpersonal sensitivity, such as increased vigilance for major relationship disruptions (i.e., threats of separation and abandonment, vigilance for relationship "intruders," sensitivity to rejection) and concomitant excessive concern about the relationship partner's availability and dependability. Applying this approach to the study of adult abusive males, moreover, has indicated that those who had physically assaulted their wives reported greater levels of both interpersonal dependency and spouse-specific dependency than maritally discordant but nonviolent males and happily married nonviolent males (Murphy, Meyer, & O'Leary, 1994). Specifically, insecure models may heighten the adults' ten-

dencies to react with extreme anger, anxiety, or both when significant relationships are perceived as being threatened. A spousal
batterer's violent outburst toward his partner may be precipitated
by perceived threats to the relationship (e.g., as evidenced by
jealousy of other males the partner has casually and innocently
interacted with), with the relationship violence signifying a protest
behavior against the imagined injury, an attachment-maintaining
behavior, or both to prevent actual separation or abandonment.

To summarize, early attachment and child maltreatment experiences inform the child that intimate relationships may involve (a)
stark power differentials where power assertion and abuse are viable
(even desirable) relationship maintenance, communication, and
conflict resolution strategies; (b) anger and fear as emotional back-
drops to relationships; and (c) negative attitudes toward others, for
example, viewing others in terms of being threatening, abandoning,
and not trustworthy.

Life Lessons

Considering the above theoretical orientation, we now identify
some of the most salient specific psychological processes that may be
operative in individuals from at-risk backgrounds: learning to abuse
power (e.g., using rage outbursts as an intimidation tactic) and
learning to fear others (e.g., lack of interpersonal trust; sensitivity
to rejection, expecting abandonment and hurt in relationships).

Life Lesson 1: Learning to Abuse Power

A key construct in understanding interpersonal violence is the
power imbalance necessary for abusive behavior and victimization
to occur (Dutton, 1994; Pence & Paymar, 1993; Walker, 1989).
Intimate relationships, such as parent and child or husband and
wife, can be grounded in rigid power structures, leading ultimately
to abuse of power. The process of intergenerational transmission of
abuse and the cycle of violence may be fundamentally about the
transmission of a power-abusive interactional style, in which a
legitimate means of handling irritability, anger, and other strong

negative affective states is for the more powerful person to "take out" on the less powerful, with an accompanying "role reversal" mind-set of the less powerful being expected to "take care of" the more powerful person.

Clinical reports identify that partner-assaultive males tend to label many emotional states as anger, and it is in the midst of high arousal (interpreted by spouse victims as rage) that violent episodes occur (Dutton, 1992). This rapid engagement of mobilizing anger has been proposed as a factor in child physical abuse as well (Milner, 1993). Furthermore, it is argued that the association of high levels of anger and violence is bolstered by the lack of verbal skills and verbal assertiveness of violent-prone individuals (Dutton, 1992). In other words, not being able to effectively "talk" it out, abusive individuals "act" it out, using violent actions to regain control. Considering the function of anger, then, explosive displays of anger become a chief means by which power is asserted and an imbalance of power is maintained. The display of rage, frightening in and of itself, becomes a power tool because, experientially, it has been associated with physical injury (Pence & Paymar, 1993; Wolfe, Wekerle, Reitzel-Jaffe, & Gough, 1995).

Two main adaptational strategies identified by Crittenden and Ainsworth (1989) to the attachment dilemmas created by abusive parenting (i.e., compulsive compliance and overt resistance) both have extreme power differentials at their base. Compulsive compliance is associated with an internal model of the other as powerful and hostile, and a self model as lovable and worthy only when compliant, with the emotional underlay of anxiety and repressed anger in relationships. Overt resistance is associated with an internal model of the other as negative, and a self model as including justifiable anger. In terms of relationship violence, overt anger may characterize the victimizer role, with displaced and denied anger characterizing the victim role.

Not surprisingly, power issues are frequently described by male batterers attending treatment programs. Batterers interpret female independence as a loss of their control, leading them to persuade or coerce their spouse into adopting his definition of relationship structure and function (Dutton & Browning, 1988). For example, domestically violent couples engage in interactions in which the husband makes increased demands for power or authority in the context of spousal withdrawal more often than do nonviolent distressed or control couples (Babcock, Waltz, Jacobson, & Gottman, 1993). In such contexts, the batterer's violent outbursts may have the rewarding function for the male of stopping the aversiveness inherent in losing a verbal conflict, restoring feelings of efficacy and control, and a cathartic expression of anger (Dutton, 1994).

The goal of power assertion may be strongly related to the psychological mechanisms known as external locus of control and projection. In the case of relationship violence, these processes result in blaming the partner for almost everything unpleasant. The theoretical function of projection and external locus of control is that unacceptable impulses and thoughts are placed on others (e.g., not accepting personal ownership of problems), and thereby the threat to a weak self-concept is neutralized (Dutton, 1994). There is empirical support for abusive persons to have an external locus of control, in which other persons and situations are blamed for problems in favor of acknowledging personal contribution and responsibility (Milner & Chilamkurti, 1991). This externality is also found across generations. Examining interactional data across four generations, Elder, Caspi, and Downey (1986) found that parents with irritable, unstable personalities tended to experience greater marital tension. When this constellation of negative factors also led to more irritable and punitive parenting, the children were more irritable and explosive; however, when the negative personal states were not expressed in an aversive style of parenting, few negative child effects were noted.

Life Lesson 2: Learning to Fear Others—
Expecting Rejection, Abandonment, and Harm

Social cognitive processes (e.g., Bandura, 1989; Strassberg & Dodge, 1995) are central in the child's learning through observation and interaction with their adult models of relationship. In addition to reenacting violent model-consistent roles, maltreatment experiences may tint the type of information given preferential processing, described by Bowlby (1980) as perceptual vigilance. Compared to nonmaltreated children, maltreated children recall a greater number of distracting aggressive stimuli (Reider & Cicchetti, 1989) and of unresolved interadult anger (Cummings, Hennessy, Rabideau, & Cicchetti, 1994). Bugental (1993) advances that maltreatment predisposes individuals toward approaching interactions with a heightened tendency to process threat. Although adaptive in the violent environment, this rapid processing of aggressive stimuli may lead to preemptive "retaliatory" or "protective" responses, intense affective reactions, and distorted perceptions and interpretations of the other interactant's behavior, for example.

As reviewed earlier, both child abuse victims and adult perpetrators of violence exhibit greater levels of aggression than controls. Furthermore, when given vignettes as stimuli for interpersonal responding, partner-assaultive males respond with greater anger and less verbal competence particularly when themes of abandonment, rejection, and jealousy are present (e.g., Holzworth-Munroe & Anglin, 1991). Assaultive partners also perceive themselves to have less decision-making power, likely enhancing the perception that physical aggression is the only effective means of ending the conflict or asserting a dominant position in the argument (Babcock et al., 1993).

Life Lesson 3:
What's Love Got to Do With It?

The indexes of "love," such as positive communication, shared attention, and warmth, are important to consider in interpersonal violence, especially when child maltreatment is viewed as a risk factor. Research on maltreated children and adolescents clearly shows that in interactions with their parents, these children receive less verbal interaction, less approval, less instruction, less shared play (e.g., Kavanaugh, Youngblade, Reid, & Fagot, 1988), and less reasoning during conflict situations (e.g., Oldershaw, Walters, & Hall, 1986; Trickett & Susman, 1988). Similarly, research on violent adolescents shows that the caretaking interactions of violent adolescents are marked by low rates of positive emotional expression and communication (e.g., Greenberg et al., 1993; Loeber, Weissman, & Reid, 1983). In return, teens who have physically assaulted their own caregivers report unrewarding family relations and low levels of feelings of parental closeness (Paulson, Coombs, & Landsverk, 1990).

Thus, expressions of intimacy and positive communication emerge as two critical features that are absent or minimal in violent relationships. Again, this empirical theme finds a parallel in the attachment literature, where maternal warmth and sensitivity is consistently associated with secure attachments and positive child behaviors and adjustment (e.g., Ainsworth et al., 1978; Bowlby, 1969/1982). Violent homes, as one would expect, directly or indirectly teach children to abuse power, to use power-assertive methods of control, and to expect others to use similar methods to maintain a relationship. Few opportunities are provided for learning interpersonal warmth and the use of positive control strategies, such as negotiation. This lack of positive relationship training clearly extends to social dating and sexual relationships during adolescence. For example, college dating partners identify that both females' and males' reports of male violence toward the female partner are significantly related to low levels of positive communication (Follette & Alexander, 1992).

Disturbingly, men who sexually aggress against women show even more pronounced communication distortions. Such men perceive women's communication in a prejudicial, suspicious fashion, based on underlying beliefs that guide their perceptions of women generally. Such "suspicious schemas" (Malamuth & Brown, 1994) impart an attitude of disbelief and disregard for the woman's attempts at communication about romantic or sexual interest, because "women don't tell the truth when it comes to sex" (Follette & Alexander, 1992, p. 701). Whereas nonsexually aggressive men feel it is even easier to read a woman's communication when it is more intense (i.e., if she is highly hostile or highly seductive), sexually aggressive men are prone to question why her reactions are so strong and discount her statements even further (Malamuth & Brown, 1994). Because perceptions are the first element in the interactive process, they are likely to play a primary role in activating and shaping future interactions (Fiske & Taylor, 1993).

The Social Context:
Challenges and Opportunities

The study of relationship violence among peerships and partnerships is still in the early stages and particularly so for the study of adolescent intimate partnerships. Nonetheless, the trend that emerges is a "what went around, goes around" pattern of relationship violence, as evidenced by greater aggression toward and victimization by peers and partners. This duality in relationship roles (victim and victimizer) raises some interesting questions for developmental processes to address because clearly at the adult level, the male is the primary assaulter and the female is overwhelmingly the victim in violent intimate adult relations, wherein the male "drives" an adult domestically violent system (Hotaling & Sugarman, 1986).

Learning to Relate: The Importance of Peers and the Emergence of Gender Differences

---

BOX 5.2

"What young people value more than anything else are relationships. They want good interpersonal ties and they want to be loved. The contest isn't even close" (Bibby & Posterski, 1992, p. 9).

Children's Play and the
Formation of Gender Beliefs

From a very early age, children have a need to organize information about their social world and form an impression of how they fit into it. Naturally, these early beliefs about the world around them are strongly influenced by what they see on a daily and routine basis: men have lawnmowers, women have baby carriages; men play baseball, women play piano. Such early views of one's world help the child to make sense of the many confusing bits of information they come into contact with each day. This process of gender identification begins early in children's lives, and gender becomes part of who they are (Beal, 1994). How this process can lead to possible sex-role *stereotypes*, however, is an issue that deserves attention, because such stereotypes can carry forward into adolescence to serve as a template for what one expects from his or her dating partner.

As any parent can attest, children are not passive recipients of gender-role stereotypes; rather, they actively observe the world around them, notice that males and females do different things, figure out their own gender assignment, and then alter their behavior accordingly. Their behavior may at times be puzzling—they may insist that men cannot be nurses or women cannot be doctors, but have no rational explanation for this argument; they may assume that their own gender is superior, simply because they identify with that gender.

These sometimes rigidly held beliefs can be explained on the basis of "gender schemas." According to developmental psychologists, cognitive structures (or *schemas*) are organized around the assumption that the sexes are different, and thereby influence how children view their social world. Such schemas, or conceptual maps, develop readily during childhood because *gender is predictive.* That is, it is easy for a child to recognize those tasks most commonly done by men or by women and, therefore, gender becomes a simple way of assigning expectations and roles (Serbin et al., 1993). If the child sees that most childcare workers, housekeepers, and grocery store shoppers are women, for example, he or she easily comprehends that these are the tasks that women do (which seems to be much more powerful than what their parents may *tell them* women can do).

As these schemas develop, they turn into beliefs and expectations about the world, thereby serving to increase the child's convictions that males and females do different things. Naturally, they are motivated to figure out what is appropriate for their own gender while being careful to avoid behaviors associated with the other gender.

Speaking Different Languages:
Status Versus Connection

BOX 5.3

"Little girls learn to split their consciousness, filtering their dreams and ambitions through boy characters while admiring the clothes of the princess. The more privileged and daring can dream of becoming exceptional women in a man's world—Smurfettes. The others are being taught to accept the more usual fate, which is to be a passenger car drawn through life by masculine train engines. Boys, who are rarely confronted with stories in which males play only minor roles, learn a simpler lesson: Girls just don't matter much" (Pollitt, 1991, p. 22).

Gender identification is a seemingly universal process that most children undertake to make more sense of their worlds, which results in the formation of a flexible or inflexible template for the formation of early peer relationships. But how can this relatively harmless process of gender identification lead to the formation of rigid sex-role expectations and gender-based beliefs among some individuals, prompting them to behave in a more or less predictable, gender-defined manner? Are some of the roots of abusive behavior and victimization evident in the patterns of play that form very early on among children of the same and opposite sex?

The process of language and speech formation develops concurrently with gender identification through interactions with parents and peers, and forms the background for one's general perceptions of others. This interpersonal phenomenon, observed by psycholinguists and anthropologists alike, is a reflection of how young children see their worlds, and how they must carefully "learn to talk" in a manner that strengthens their same-sex identification. A close look at this process, referred to as "gender-lex" (Tannen, 1991), reveals some of the cognitive foundations underlying significant differences in how boys and girls form and refine their view of same- and opposite-sex relationships.

When observing the speech and play patterns of young children, researchers have discovered that very different processes are at work for boys than for girls (e.g., Lever, 1978). When boys are at play with other boys, their games and language reflect the importance of status and independence. Boys tend to play outside in larger groups that are hierarchically formed. They choose or form a leader, and are likely to challenge one another as to "expertise" or leadership ability by giving orders or telling stories and jokes. Their play activity is often centered on having "winners" and "losers," with rules that are carefully monitored (and argued). During such play, boys are more likely than girls to boast of their skills and make an issue over who is "best."

Girls' play activities are qualitatively and structurally different from those of boys. Girls are more likely to play in pairs or small groups, with person(s) they consider as "best friends." For girls, intimacy and closeness are primary, and therefore one's "standing" in the group is determined by their degree of relative closeness or connectedness to the others. Noticeably, their games are less likely to have winners or losers—they choose to play house or make crafts—and girls who excel at the chosen activity are expected not to brag. Rather than giving orders or forming hierarchies, they make suggestions to one another (e.g., "Let's do this;" "How about that"). Girls are less likely to challenge one another or jockey for status; rather, their activities reflect a clear preference for spending time together while sitting and talking.

The ways young boys and girls play sheds considerable light on their relationship preferences, revealing what Tannen (1991) refers to as a paradox of independence and intimacy: Boys tend to focus more on status—who's giving orders and who's taking them, being on the lookout for signs of being told what to do. Girls, on the other hand, are centered more on intimacy—monitoring their friendships for subtle shifts in alliance, and feeling some sense of "status" by being connected to a group of friends.

Interestingly, the Chinese identified a similar phenomenon many centuries ago (Duerk, 1989). They recognized that women (who are grounded in the Yin), are faced with an eternal paradox because of the differing nature of Yin from Yang. Whereas the nature of Yin (receptive) is to yield, the nature of Yang is to press forward (to dominate). Yet the Chinese considered the two forces to be intrinsically equal and necessary to achieve balance. Thus, although the masculine process has so often seemed the superior, the feminine process is as much needed for wholeness as the masculine process (Duerk, 1989).

Adults too learn their style of interpersonal communication through such peer interchanges, and it is therefore not surprising that male and female styles are very different. Each style is valid in its own right, although dissatisfaction is bound to occur as one's interest in communicating with the opposite sex increases during early adolescence. For example, it is common for adolescent boys to complain that girls are trying to "curb my freedom," whereas adolescent girls complain that boys refuse to talk about personal or intimate topics.

The developmental consequences of these gender-specific communication styles are vast. For example, a common stereotype is that women's language is *powerless*—if you're not one up, then you're one down (Cline, 1989). In fact, women's language styles are more *indirect but not powerless;* such a style is very effective in communicating with other women, but may be seen by men as powerless or indecisive (Tannen, 1991).

Unfortunately, over time it becomes easy for members of each gender to attribute these stylistic differences to "personality flaws" or generalized intentions on the part of the opposite sex to frustrate or impede one's preferred way of relating (i.e., "men are distant"; "women are intrusive"). Such beliefs, in the absence of objective knowledge or new learning experiences, set the stage for continued projection of blame on the other partner and the risk of escalating conflict. Tannen (1991) suggests, however, that such conflicts can be resolved by women learning from men to accept conflict without feeling a threat to intimacy, and by men learning from women to accept interdependence without feeling a threat to their freedom.

These important communication principles can be most effectively taught to individuals who are motivated to learn and who have not as yet established rigid, global attributions of blame. Again, adolescence provides an excellent training opportunity for learning and rehearsal of these positive, nonblaming skills of communication.

Peer Groupings

Vulnerable youth have disrupted peer relationships, both in terms of heightened aggressivity toward peers and their affiliation with a deviant peer group. From a young age, maltreated children can be distinguished from their nonmaltreated counterparts on the basis of their aggressive behavior toward peers (Main & George, 1985), as well as their propensity to be rejected by their peers (Salzinger, Feldman, Hammer, & Rosario, 1993). In addition, maltreated children are more likely to appraise the intentions of others in an unrealistic or distorted fashion. That is, they interpret ambiguous comments or behavior as being a possible threat that demands a preemptive strike. This hostile attributional style, developed perhaps as a coping reaction to their own maltreatment, reappears during interactions both with peers (Dodge, Bates, & Petit, 1990) and parents (Herzberger, Potts, & Dillon, 1981).

Other evidence that maltreated children are strongly "tuned in" and affected by violence is the finding that maltreated children report greater fear following exposure to interadult anger (Hennessy, Rabideau, Cicchetti, & Cummings, 1994). Such emotional reactivity is likely a function of repeated incidents of "conditioning," in which arousal and fear are paired with loud voices, facial expressions, certain topics of conversation, and similar circumstances that alert them to the possibility of conflict. As one would expect, such children grow up displaying a heightened sense of vigilance and emotional overreactivity to others. Consequently, youths from violent and abusive homes are reported by teachers as exhibiting more aggressive behavior, hostility toward others, and sexual harassment than youths without such a history (Wolfe, Wekerle, Reitzel-Jaffe, & Lefebvre, 1995).

Understandably, these cognitive, emotional, and behavioral learning experiences within the family are powerful influences on the formation of one's social network and social goals. At-risk and vulnerable youths are more likely to associate with delinquent peers and engage in antisocial behaviors (Patterson, DeBaryshe, & Ramsey, 1989), which further serves to impair their ability to master important developmental tasks. Moreover, such associations perpetuate attitudes, motivations, emotions, and beliefs that encourage the likelihood of coercive behavior. That is, the proviolent network of vulnerable adolescents reinforces their primary frame of reference and often "empowers" the youth toward an increasingly violent lifestyle. Similarly, one's social goals or expectancies about relationships are formed on the basis of previous peer and family experiences, which in turn influence our choice of problem-solving methods (Rubin & Krasnor, 1986).

The social goals of these youth, not surprisingly, are defined by a high value for dominance and revenge and a low value for affiliation (Lochman, Wayland, & White, 1993). If unabated, this developmental course, combined with added cultural stereotypes for men and women, may lead to both sexual and nonsexual forms of acting out during adolescence and young adulthood to control and coerce others (Dutton, 1994; Malamuth et al., 1991).

Interestingly, however, the strength, dramatic content, and general attractiveness of a violent lifestyle has not always been fully recognized as to its impact on young adults. For example, illegal and self-destructive adolescent risk-taking behaviors (such as unprotected, unmoderated sexual activity; delinquency; illicit drug activity) may, at least in the early stages, have the effect of *increasing* the youth's self-esteem (Kaplan, Johnson, Bailey, & Simon, 1987; McCord, 1990). This maladaptive, yet empowering, process is superimposed on the normal risk-taking behaviors of adolescence, where experimentation is seen as a necessary step toward competency and confidence in attaining autonomy, mastery, and intimacy goals (Baumrind, 1987). The maltreated child and adolescent is preequipped to form peer relationships that are defined by an excessive degree of cautiousness, status, and power at their core. Simply stated, violence becomes reinforcing because one feels powerful and more effective at getting others to do what you want, when you want it.

Social Dating:
The Testing Ground

Social dating relationships that emerge during adolescence may represent a transition point between one's own experiences of nurturance and care as a child and the future likelihood of becoming abusive or being abused as an adult (Bethke & DeJoy, 1993). For this reason, social dating may be a primary "testing ground" of one's acquired ability to express emotion and receive affection without resorting to abusive practices or submitting to attempts at coercion or intimidation by a dating partner. Because adolescents like to "try on" different roles and actions, social dating experiences are often emblematic of one's exposure to various conflict resolution tactics, role models, and learning opportunities.

As one would expect, individuals who have been exposed to healthy models are more likely to approach dating with greater self-confidence, problem-solving ability, and personal options; conversely, youths who have grown up with psychological and physical forms of violence, and who lack any suitable alternative role models or experiences, are most likely to enter the social dating arena with power-based expectations about the conduct of one's self and partner.

For instance, studies demonstrate that youths who grew up in violent homes have a greater likelihood of becoming offenders as well as victims of personal violence (Kalmuss, 1984; Wolfe, Wekerle, Reitzel-Jaffe, & Gough, 1995). In particular, dating violence during adolescence, combined with a past history of violence in the family of origin (i.e., physical abuse, wife abuse, or both) are strong prerelationship predictors of intimate violence in early adulthood and marriage (Murphy et al., 1994; O'Leary, Malone, & Tyree, 1994).

The pathway between violence in the home and violence in social dating relationships is by no means straightforward and inevitable, however. Armed with suitable problem resolution skills or strong motivation to avoid violence and achieve intimacy, many youths are capable of escaping this neck of the funnel, especially when provided with positive opportunities to learn about healthy relationships. For this reason, social dating experiences provide the youth with excellent opportunities to acquire and rehearse interpersonal communication and problem-solving skills that will carry forward to future long-term relationships. Many of the challenges inherent in dating relationships, moreover, are typical of things to come (rather than particularly unique to adolescent relationships); therefore, successful resolution or positive growth in response to these challenges is a major achievement of young adulthood.

One of the most notable challenges facing adolescent peer and dating relationships is conflict resolution. Conflicts are normal, although not necessarily severe, among all youth. In an expansive literature review, Laursen and Collins (1994) conclude that teens have an average of seven disagreements per day, which vary considerably with the person with whom they are having a problem. Mothers come in first, followed by siblings, friends, and romantic partners. Fathers, other peers, and other adults follow far behind. Of importance is the finding that negative affect is highest during conflicts involving family members, other adults, and peer associates; however, negative affect is not characteristic of adolescent disputes with friends or romantic partners. During conflicts with dating partners, girls are likely to show increasing emphasis on compromise rather than submission; boys, on the other hand, rely almost exclusively on submission of one or both parties to resolve such disputes.

With *vulnerable* adolescents and their romantic partners, however, these normative gender differences seem to be taken much further into a violent dimension. The potential for a violent dynamic in adolescent relationships increases significantly from middle to late adolescence for both males and females, as a function of increased jealousy and conflict (Feiring, 1995).

Teasing is another important feature of the social life of adolescents, and one of the most commonly reported fears of high school students (Schaefer, 1978). Most often, teasing involves "making fun" of the target, especially about some characteristic that deviates from the group norm (e.g., "fat," "ugly"), which can escalate to the point of indignation. Some less common forms of verbal (e.g., sarcastic comments, tricking the target, and so on) and nonverbal teasing (e.g., pointing, making faces, keeping a possession from the owner) can be especially upsetting to the target. Although there are playful and beneficial aspects of teasing, much teasing occurs as a power-oriented interaction in which a more powerful individual dominates a less assertive or less powerful one (Shapiro, Baumeister, & Kessler, 1991). Drawing on this parallel, teasing can be considered as belonging to the same class of behavior as coercive and openly hostile forms of abuse. For this reason it warrants consideration as an "entry-level" behavior for those inclined to dominate others as they form their own intimate relationships.

Teasing may play an important role in the development of cross-gender relationships and, as such, may signal the transition into heterosexual relationships, the abuse of power, or both. For example, such behavior allows the teaser to approach and interact with an attractive member of the opposite sex while at the same time denying that any interest exists (Sluckin, 1981). Similarly, Shapiro et al. (1991) explain that as children approach puberty there is often a change from teasing about the *presence* of heterosexual interest to teasing about the *absence* of such interest.

Because it is a common rite of passage, most teasing does not escalate into violence; however, teasing holds attractive opportunities for the teaser as a means of camouflaging his or her intentions and expressing sentiments that could not otherwise be expressed. For example, there is a false perception on the part of the teaser to see his or her motive as benign and friendly, whereas the target experiences teasing as hostile and painful. Teasing combines the elements of aggression, humor, and ambiguity in such a manner that permits the teaser to elicit a range of both affective responses (e.g., laughter, tears) and behavioral responses (e.g., joking to physical assault; Shapiro et al., 1991), and therefore represents one of the important developmental challenges accompanying the formation of dating relationships.

Finally, we turn to the emergence of gender-specific violence, especially among vulnerable adolescents from violent homes. Although studies of the connection between child maltreatment and violence in dating relationships are few, important trends are emerging. Based on a high school sample of 340 adolescents, for example, our research team found that males who were more physically and verbally abusive toward dating partners, as well as females who were more abused, were significantly more likely to have come from harsh and abusive family backgrounds. Males, in particular, who came from abusive families and who also lacked a secure, positive image of themselves in relationships were most at risk for dating violence (Wekerle, Wolfe, & Lefebvre, 1995).

This gender-specific result may be understood in the light of recent research suggesting that abusive behavior is primarily learned through the same-sex parent (Davis & Allen, 1995), identifying that males would be most detrimentally affected by being victimized by their father figure(s) and witnessing male assaults of their mothers. In our high school sample, 12% of the males reported witnessing domestic violence and 35% reported being the victim of severe physical abuse (e.g., choked/burned/scalded; kicked/bit/punched; physically attacked; threatened with severe harm).

The Vulnerable Individual

Individual differences pertaining to cognitive, personality, and physical capabilities are relevant to the cycle of violence, because some of these dimensions may make one more vulnerable to becoming a victim or offender. Although researchers have not been able to isolate reliable psychological or biological variables associated with a propensity toward intimate violence (Dutton, 1994), child and adult characteristics that have received initial empirical support are considered. These characteristics generally fall into two categories—anger control problems and developmental psychopathology—that contribute toward an individual's increased likelihood of violence.

Problems in Anger
Expression and Control

Part of the child's coping with parental conflict or maltreatment includes managing the angry affect elicited from the generally frustrating and sometimes fear-inducing caregiving and interactional patterns (Davies & Cummings, 1994). Research suggests that abused children either learn to inhibit and, ultimately, deny feelings of anger by adopting a stance of compulsive compliance and servitude to others, or they may fail to make such a transition and remain negative and resistant (Crittenden & Ainsworth, 1989). Thus, risk of anger modulation problems in the context of intimate relationships would be expected for those with a history of maltreatment. Emerging evidence supports this view: Maltreated toddlers (Beeghly & Cicchetti, 1994) as well as school-aged children (Shields, Cicchetti, & Ryan, 1994) show emotional regulation difficulties accompanied by poor verbal skills for describing their own internal affective states. Much less is known, however, of the socioemotional development of adolescents who have experienced maltreatment (Wolfe & McGee, 1994).

Gender differences are clearly evident both in relation to the actual expression of anger, and in its intended and perceived effect on the other partner. For example, based on a sample of 60 adult couples experiencing husband-to-wife domestic violence, Jacobson et al. (1994) found men to be more domineering and more defensive with their partners, and less likely to acknowledge a problem with their style of relating. The women, in contrast, showed more tension, fear, and sadness during conflict situations involving their male partners. The researchers highlight this important gender difference in how violence functions in the relationship: Whereas both partners engage in frequent use of coercive and abusive tactics, only male violence produces fear in the partner. This finding, in turn, accounts for the ability of men to use violence as a means of psychological and social control.

Researchers and clinicians (e.g., Dutton, 1994; Gondolf, 1985) have also theorized that violent men have difficulty acknowledging and expressing feelings other than anger, and that men in general are more likely to label any form of arousal as anger. Such lack of skill in expressing emotion, it is reasoned, results in chronic feelings of frustration and increased likelihood of violent means to attain greater control in the relationship (Dutton & Strachan, 1987; Holtzworth-Munroe, 1992). This view is congruent with the descriptions provided by battered women of their partners, in which anger and jealousy are frequently mentioned as instigating factors. Jealousy produces a range of behavioral responses, such as aggression and increased vigilance, as well as affective reactions, such as rage and depression (Dutton, 1994). Moreover, sexual jealousy (a form of expressing power and control) is one of the most commonly reported features of the battering relationship (Walker, 1989).

Developmental Psychopathology

Borderline Personality Organization

One personality cluster that has been identified as a possible etiological factor is borderline-antisocial personality traits (Dutton, 1994; Else, Wonderlich, Beatty, Christie, & Staton, 1994). Although few batterers meet the full diagnostic criteria, there is the suggestion that batterers display borderline personality organization (BPO), which includes a proclivity toward rule violations, irresponsibility, affective instability, and relationship difficulties (Dutton, 1995). These traits, moreover, overlap with the features of the three-stage model of battering episodes described by Walker (1979) in her classic portrayal of the Battered Woman's Syndrome.

The first stage of battering is said to be characterized by "tension building" (Walker, 1979). The equivalent borderline personality phenomenon is described as chronic dysphoria and frustration in relationships, due to unmet intimacy needs in the context of nonexistent skills to negotiate demands for intimacy. The second battering stage is considered to be triggered by a seemingly irrelevant, trivial, or both external event or the internal state of the man. Again, a parallel can be drawn to BPO, in which the perceived threat of relationship loss, accompanied by defensive maneuvers such as anger, rage, and projection (e.g., active devaluation of the significant other) culminate in a battering episode. The final "reparation" phase is triggered by the need to ward off subjective experience of aloneness and to reestablish an emotional commitment from the partner to the relationship, culminating in various appeasement and "winning over" behaviors (e.g., promises to reform, tokens of affection, confessionals, and so on). Once the batterer perceives that the relationship has been resolidified, the above phases are likely to be repeated in a "push/pull" or "approach/avoidance" manner to relationships.

Efforts to categorize subtypes of assaultive males suggest that a third of assaulters could be classified along such BPO dimensions (Saunders, 1992). Although BPO conceptualizations have been applied to adult domestic violence, these traits have not been investigated among adolescents at risk for relationship violence.

Posttraumatic Stress Symptomatology

Interestingly, recent research suggests that posttraumatic stress disorder (PTSD) may also characterize interpersonally violent adult males, and is also a useful paradigm for understanding childhood experiences of maltreatment (Wekerle & Wolfe, in press). Again, however, we find that adolescents have been missed as a possible group at risk for such problems. Dutton (1994), for example, has postulated a central role of trauma symptomatology as a mediator for underlying psychological processes linking childhood maltreatment and adult partner-assaultive behavior. Dutton (1995) found that assaultive males report more chronic trauma symptoms than nonabusive controls, and trauma symptomatology is associated with frequent anger and emotional abuse of the partner. Furthermore, he found that abusive early experiences (parental rejection, abuse) accounted for 26% of the variance in the adult batterers' trauma symptomatology, thereby suggesting that trauma symptomatology may flow from violence in childhood, as well as may facilitate the perpetration of violence in adulthood.

Depressive Symptomatology

Partner-assaultive men also score higher on self-critical scales (Else et al., 1994), suggesting that they experience more chronic states of dysphoria associated with, for example, self-critical depression (Blatt & Homann, 1992). Such signs of depression may be a consequence of the PTSD symptomatology (i.e., heightened irritability and dysphoria), although the exact mechanisms are not known.

Chronic dysphoria/irritability, when accompanied by low tolerance for stress and low levels of potential buffers (e.g., social support, social competence), serves to predispose the male toward striking out violently. For example, abusive parents become more physiologically aroused to child-related aversive states, such as a child crying, than nonabusive parents (McCanne & Milner, 1991). Thus, it appears that abuse-prone adults experience more aversive affect, such as anger and irritability. Consequently, aggression toward intimates may serve the function of dissipating tension, anxiety, physical discomfort, and dysphoria/dissatisfaction (Dutton, 1995).

Not surprisingly, male batterers report greater acting-out hostility than controls (Else et al., 1994). This low frustration/stress tolerance view is bolstered further by evidence showing greater substance use among abusive and at-risk adults (Milner & Chilamkurti, 1991), where a motivation for substance use may also be stress reduction. Indeed, alcohol consumption is one of the most common commitants of adult violence (Famularo, Kinscherff, & Fenton, 1992) as well as teen relationship violence (Girshick, 1993).

In closing, it is useful to consider how these identified traits of abusers can be integrated to explain their behavior more fully. Dutton and Golant (1995) identify three primary elements that come together to structure the personality of the repeat abuser: a shaming, emotionally rejecting father or an absent father; an insecure attachment to mother; and the experience of seeing or hearing violence in the family as a child. These elements combine to create a fragile sense of self in the boy and the man, which is the underlying feature of the abusive personality. The only time such a man feels whole is when he is beating his partner. Thus, abusive men share several behavioral characteristics in common: problems with anger, inability to trust, delusional jealousy, a tendency to blame others for their feelings and behavior, recurring moods, and PTSD symptoms.

Prevention Possibilities

The above theoretical description of the development of relationship violence, which we have likened to a funneling process leading to greater risk for some vulnerable youth, contains by implication several worthwhile directions for violence prevention. Although some of the powerful cultural and familial forces will require generations to resolve, there are practical steps that can be taken at present to begin this process. Especially relevant for the needs of today's youth, however, are some of the straightforward educational experiences that are suspected or known to attenuate the negative influence of the factors noted in our model. For example, the broader social and cultural negative influences could be ameliorated by increasing access to community resources, public education and awareness about violence, antiviolence education in schools, social action efforts by youth to promote antiviolence information, and values of cooperation and mutual support. We touch on some of the broader issues pertaining to protective factors and innovative programs here, and provide more details on practical strategies in the following chapter.

To counter values of individualism and competitiveness with values of cooperation and mutual support, youth can be empowered to oppose the various forms of violence and oppression that surround them. The active agent in empowerment is participation, and a cooperative peer model encourages youth to support one another while providing a venue to model positive attitudes and values.

Given our focus on relationship development, efforts to create "new" healthy relationship opportunities may be a prime intervention target. The power of positive relationships, for example, has been shown to relate to child resilience and their ability to break out of the cycle of violence. Many individuals can "make up for lost ground" by developing healthy relationships, often outside of the original family system, such as with a supportive partner or friend (e.g., Davis & Allen, 1995). Intervention studies involving mothers who had difficult family histories (e.g., maltreatment) have also found that engaging in a responsive, supportive relationship enables them to become a secure and stable force for their children, avoiding the aversive and violent parenting that they themselves had received (e.g., Lyons-Ruth, Connell, Grunebaum, & Botein, 1990; Olds, in press; Wolfe, 1991). New relationship opportunities, then, seem to provide vulnerable youth with a "second chance" at intervening and, hopefully, breaking the intergenerational transmission of violence. These possibilities are explored throughout the remainder of this book.

CHAPTER SIX

Applying the Principles

Core Ingredients of Successful Prevention Programs

BOX 6.1

"Initially, adolescents explore potentially damaging activities tentatively. They are tried on for size. Before damaging patterns are firmly established, there is a major and badly neglected opportunity for intervention to prevent casualties throughout the lifespan. This is best done by meeting fundamental requirements for healthy adolescent development" (Hamburg, Millstein, Mortimer, Nightingale, & Petersen, 1993, p. 386).

The infiltration of violence in our society seems at times to be irrevocably woven into the fabric of our culture. Sadly, many individuals who are most in need of preventive interventions already have multiple problems. As Jessor (1993) notes, problems come in packages and often cannot be treated in isolation. Individuals at the bottom of the "funnel," we recognize, are not only at risk for becoming the victims or perpetrators of violence; most often they

115

are also at risk for criminality, school drop-out or unemployment, substance abuse, early pregnancy, and a variety of other health compromising outcomes.

Given the complexity and immensity of this issue, we need to consider a few basic and important parameters that guide as well as restrict our plans and expectations. First, we have to realize that each individual has a lengthy background already established by the time most prevention efforts get underway. What can we expect from a program, therefore, that occupies only a small percentage of an individual's time, and which must overcome years of prior "training?"

Second, prevention is likely never to receive the priority and funding that is necessary to demonstrate a long-term benefit adequately. How can we rally our limited resources most effectively, and convince others that the effort is worthwhile?

Third, as emphasized throughout this book, violence in relationships develops over time and is affected by many interconnected layers of influence. Where should we focus our efforts, therefore, to have the most impact—on the community, the neighborhood, the school, the peer group, the family, or the individual?

Finally, we need to acknowledge that our understanding of violence in relationships is still emerging, and our tools for affecting change are somewhat primitive. Therefore, what are the most effective strategies for producing change (based on other areas of study), and to whom should we direct these efforts?

The purpose of the next two chapters is to respond to some of these questions by translating the theory behind prevention into concrete recommendations for promoting change. The prevention of personal violence is an approachable goal that is well worth pursuing, especially in light of the very limited and costly alternatives. How we choose to go about meeting our prevention goals may still be in the formative stages. The state of knowledge, however, has progressed to a level whereby we can pinpoint many of the important ingredients of promoting change and narrow our efforts more specifically.

In the first section, current knowledge is presented about the process of change and strategies that bring about desired change.

Change is not a one-step process; rather, it requires a combination of educational, skill developmental, and experiential, action-based strategies that is most likely to prompt someone to make changes and to maintain them. The information derived from parallel efforts to promote health and prevent illness or deviant behavior across different age groups not only supports the feasibility of prevention with youth, but also generates ideas for the initiation of such efforts.

By capitalizing on the advances in related fields of prevention research, some of the fundamental and innovative behavior change principles are applied to the issue of healthy relationship formation. This brings us to the design and purpose of the Youth Relationships Project and the manner in which these principles are integrated into a health promotion strategy for youth in the final chapter.

Understanding Change: The Beginnings of Prevention and Health Promotion

Researchers and clinicians have been in the business of promoting desired change for decades, which has led to numerous theories about different underlying motivations for change. According to the longstanding psychoanalytic school of thought, change could be prompted by helping people come to a deeper understanding of their underlying conflicts and unconscious motives affecting their actions. The behaviorist school downplayed the need for self-understanding and instead developed ways to manipulate the stimuli and consequences that may control the behavior in question. Cognitive theorists then put forward the additional premise that changing how individuals think and how they attribute blame and causation would lead to changes in behavior.

Despite healthy controversy between the many different schools of psychological thought, no one theory of change has received unanimous support. Instead, studies suggest that the most successful strategy for promoting change is not one strategy at all; it involves a combination of strategies that are a best fit to the needs of the individual or group. In practice, the *quality of the therapeutic relationship* also plays an instrumental role in this process, by creating the cornerstone for examining one's options and directions for change (Herman, 1992).

Instead of reexamining the question of *what* makes people change, researchers are currently turning their attention to the question of *how* people change. Prochaska, DiClemente, and Norcross (1992), for example, assumed that if one were to identify similarities among different experiences of change, the basic, common principles underlying the structure of change could be revealed. They began by examining similarities among drug addicts who were self-initiated changers (i.e., those who had successfully countered their problem without external help) and other-directed changers (i.e., those who countered their addiction with the help of a program). Although their work has focused primarily on people who are attempting to overcome a substance addiction, their findings have important implications for the study of change and growth in the context of relationship development.

After studying change processes for several years, this research team made an important observation that led to their conception of the *spiral theory of change*. This spiral is shown in Figure 6.1. According to this model, five stages of change are continually being repeated in an upward spiraling fashion, corresponding to the additive gains being achieved by the individual over time. Thus, behavior change is a process, not a destiny or final outcome. Gains are continually being made, but setbacks and relapses are to be expected and accommodated. The emphasis is placed on gradual gains in competence and ability, rather than the termination of a particular target behavior alone or the arrest of a disease process. The major characteristics of each of these five stages, labeled precontemplation, contemplation, preparation, action, and maintenance are described here, with reference to an example involving social dating and drinking.

Precontemplation: During this initial stage of change individuals are not as yet aware, or are underaware, of their problem. Thus, they have no intention of changing their behavior. Other significant people in their lives, however, are usually aware that a change is

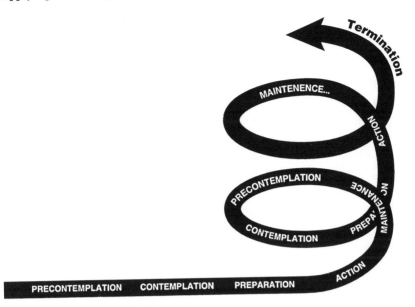

Figure 6.1. The Spiral of Change Model
SOURCE: Prochaska, J., DiClemente, C., & Norcross, J. (1992). In search of how people change. *American Psychologist, 47,* 1102-1114. Copyright © 1992 by the American Psychological Association. Reprinted with permission.

required, and are often pushing them in some fashion toward change. (For example, an adolescent male may ignore his girlfriend's pleas not to drink and drive, believing that there is nothing wrong with what he is doing.)

Contemplation: At this second stage, individuals are becoming aware that they have a problem and they begin to think seriously about doing something about it, although they have not yet committed themselves to making a change. "Contemplators" often weigh the pros and cons of their current behavior with those of the proposed change in behavior, attempting to find a simple compromise or solution. Prochaska et al. (1992) describe this stage as "knowing where you want to go but not quite ready yet" (p. 1103). (At this stage, the adolescent may have gotten into fights with his girlfriend about his drinking and driving, been involved in accidents and similar crises, or all of these. He may "let her drive" on occasion, but more to appease her than to take responsibility for change.)

Preparation: Individuals in the preparation stage are "playing" with change. Often, they have made semiserious attempts at solving their problem, either by reducing the behavior they wish to change or by eliminating it altogether for short periods of time. They have not, however, made a full commitment to change, and their behavior reflects this indecision. (The teen stops bringing drinks to the party, intending to curb his drinking; however, he will on occasion take advantage of the "hospitality" of others and still takes risks.)

Action: During this stage an individual makes the most visible and significant behavioral changes. Rather than spending time thinking about what has to change, individuals focus on taking action and look for practical ways to follow through on their intentions. (In our example, the youth may acknowledge his girlfriend's concerns and select to either take public transportation or to bring nonalcoholic beverages to the party.)

Maintenance: Stabilizing behavior change and avoiding relapse are considered to be hallmarks of maintenance. In this stage, therefore, individuals must consolidate their gains and remain committed to their choice of action. In many cases maintenance requires lifelong changes in many behaviors, not just in a particular target behavior. (For example, to stay committed to his decision not to drink and drive or to abuse alcohol, it may be necessary for our teen to change his group of friends or their typical hangout.)

At first glance, these stages seem to represent a linear pattern of change that represents a gradual, but straightforward, ascent to the goal. These researchers note, however, that individuals often make many attempts at change before they are successful. Importantly, they emphasize that *relapse is the rule rather than the exception.* Each time an individual attempts to change, he or she learns a little more and gains a little more experience, thus increasing the potential success of his or her subsequent attempts. Thus, each repetition through the five stages of change leaves individuals at a different, more advanced, point on the spiral.

We now turn to some of the more successful methods for promoting change at different stages of awareness and growth.

Promoting Change: A New Look at Prevention Strategies

To demonstrate long-term change, prevention programs need to encourage movement through all of the stages of change. Some stages, however, may require different methods of education or training than others to stimulate further growth. These methods must be identified and matched as closely as possible to the needs and level of each individual or target group.

To investigate this matching process, Prochaska et al. (1992) asked thousands of individuals in each of the precontemplation, contemplation, preparation, action, and maintenance stages of smoking cessation and weight loss how they accomplished their desired changes. Notably, individuals in the precontemplation and contemplation stages were most open to *educational techniques*, such as consciousness-raising, self-interpretation, and self-evaluation. As individuals moved toward preparation, they began to use more self- and environmental-control techniques (such as avoiding situations that increase the probability of engaging in the problem behavior), although their usage was inconsistent. By the action stage, however, individuals were consistently using effective coping and self-management strategies (i.e., not buying an addictive substance or going near known hangouts).

Based on research on how people change, we can tentatively assign a "role" to different strategies of prevention. Figure 6.2 repeats the spiral model of change with the addition of the interventions that are most likely to promote movement through the stages. Education-based prevention is likely to be most successful at raising an individual's awareness and increasing his or her knowledge about a problem, thus promoting movement from the

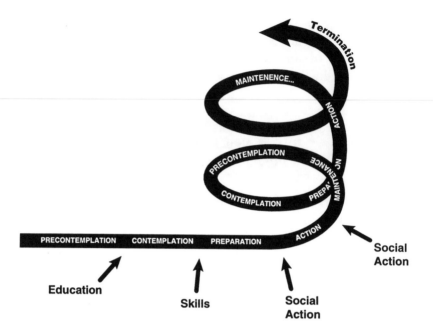

Figure 6.2. The Spiral Model of Change, Including Interventions That are Most Likely to Promote Movement Through the Stages
SOURCE: Prochaska, J., DiClemente, C., & Norcross, J. (1992). In search of how people change. *American Psychologist, 47,* 1102-1114. Copyright © 1992 by the American Psychological Association. Reprinted with permission.

precontemplation to the contemplation stage. Skills-based prevention focuses on teaching individuals ways to surmount problems, or to increase their competency in certain areas. This type of activity is most likely to shift an individual from the contemplation stage to the preparation stage. Finally, experiential, action-based prevention activities focus on putting the skills to use, often in supportive settings. This approach promotes movement from the preparation stage to the action and maintenance stages of change.

In the following sections we outline the prevention technologies associated with each of these types of intervention, and we put these into practice with the Youth Relationships Project in Chapter 7.

Education: Advancing From
Precontemplation to Contemplation

BOX 6.2

"In a high-tech industrial society, young people must learn the basic skills of reading, writing, and arithmetic to survive. If they are to thrive, they also need a fund of information about themselves and the world around them" (McWhirter, McWhirter, McWhirter, & McWhirter, 1993, p. 86).

Educational approaches to prevention show promise for developing individual knowledge, awareness and understanding of oneself. Thus, they have the potential to move individuals from the precontemplation stage of change, where they are not aware of a problem, to the contemplation stage.

Recent ideas about the role of education in prevention comes from social-cognitive theorists and social-information processing theorists, who have outlined patterns of thought that are associated with maladaptive behaviors. These perspectives have added significantly to our understanding of the "how to's" of educational efforts for prevention. Three of the most promising educational interventions involve the provision of technical information, normative information, and personalized information.

Technical Information

Technical information refers to the "basic facts" of a target behavior and its prevention, which are needed to form an awareness and understanding of the problem. To bring about changes in a particular behavior, it is necessary to provide accurate information about the nature of the problem, to provide definitions of major concepts, and to provide information to counter myths. For example, to deter youths from drug usage, it is important that they have the true facts about the drugs in question and the nature of the risks involved.

In a review of school-based drug and alcohol prevention programs, for example, Bangert-Drowns (1988) concluded that programs that provide technical information did indeed affect knowledge and attitudes about problem behaviors, although technical information by itself seldom led to corresponding changes in behavior. Child sexual abuse prevention programs have also relied considerably on informational strategies, using methods such as teaching children what sexual abuse is, increasing their awareness of who possible abusers may be, emphasizing that children have the right to control their own bodies, and stressing that children should tell a trusted adult if touched in an inappropriate manner (see Wolfe, Reppucci, & Hart, 1995, for review).

Normative Information

A relatively new approach to preventive education involves the use of normative information, such as prevalence rates, incident rates, and patterns of use to inform participants of their need to change. A recent study serves as an illustration of the relationship between normative perceptions and risk behavior. Gibbons, Helweg-Larsen, and Gerrard (1995) tested two processes that link normative information to social influence, the "false-consensus" effect and "prototype perception" effect, in relation to four adolescent risk behaviors (i.e., unprotected sexual intercourse, smoking, drug use, and drinking). Young adolescents were asked to estimate the prevalence of each of the risk behaviors (e.g., "How many people do you believe . . . "), and to give descriptions of the "typical smoker" and the "typical unwed mother." Then, they evaluated how they were similar to the described prototype.

To evaluate the relationship between risk behaviors and normative beliefs, Gibbons et al. (1995) compared the prevalence estimations of "doers" (i.e., those who were currently engaging in each of the behaviors) and the "nondoers" (i.e., those who were not engaged in the behaviors). Results show that knowledge of correct normative information was associated with a lower likelihood of engaging in high-risk behavior. For example, teens who had not been sexually active estimated that 35.2% of their peers were sexually active, whereas those who reported that they had been sexually active estimated that 66.5% of fellow teens were sexually active (almost double the estimate of the nondoers). In actual fact, only 12.4% of the sample reported that they had been sexually active. This trend of overestimation is echoed across the remaining three risk behaviors; in all cases prevalence estimates were especially exaggerated among those teens who had engaged in the specified behavior.

Donaldson, Graham, and Hansen (1994) have provided evidence that prevention programs based on normative and technical information can be successful. These researchers were concerned with discovering the most successful method of preventing the use of alcohol and drugs among teens. To investigate this question, they randomly assigned 124 elementary schools into four conditions: an information about consequences of use, resistance skills training program, a normative education program, and a combined program. Students in each condition received four 45-minute lessons in Grade 5 and a booster lesson in Grade 7.

Each program had the expected result: The education program increased knowledge, the resistance skills training program increased teens' ability to recognize and deal with peer pressure, and the normative education program reduced prevalence estimates and beliefs about acceptability of use. Long-term follow-up, however, indicated that only the normative beliefs approach consistently predicted future drug and alcohol use. Neither resistance skills nor knowledge alone were significant predictors of Grade 8 substance use. Once again, these results support the potential of normative education for prevention efforts aimed at selected groups of individuals.

Personalized Information

Individuals working within the social service field have long recognized the advantages of providing information that personalizes an issue for an individual. Persons who are further along in the change process are often asked to relate their experiences to those just beginning the process of change. In most treatment programs, considerable time and effort is spent encouraging individuals to examine the direct impact of problem behaviors, and potential changes, on their lives.

One has to be cautious when personalizing information, however, to avoid the common mistake most parents make, as reflected by the statement: "If only they understood the risks and the consequences, then they wouldn't do it." This belief holds special significance when considering an adolescent population. Our culture tends to believe that adolescents have an exaggerated sense of their own invulnerability. That is, adolescents focus on the benefits of risk behaviors, while underestimating and minimizing the associated risks. Accordingly, it is tempting to conclude that prevention should simply be a matter of emphasizing the potential harm of risk behaviors. Research suggests, however, that teens often know and understand the risks associated with their behaviors, yet they still may prefer to take risks (e.g., Quadrel, Fischhoff, & Davis, 1993). Therefore, their participation in risk behaviors can neither be attributed to a lack of knowledge, nor an exaggerated perception of individual invulnerability.

BOX 6.3
*Using Education to
Prevent Gang Involvement*

There are several exemplary educational programs currently underway, most of which are being provided in the context of the school system. One such program is the Paramount Plan: Alternatives to Gang Membership, which has been identified as a model program by the U.S. Department of Education. This program is aimed at preventing teens from becoming involved in gangs by giving 15 weeks of 55-minute presentations in all 5th grade classrooms. This is followed by 8 biweekly presentations in Grade 7 to reintroduce, reinforce, and expand on the concepts learned in Grade 5. Sessions cover issues such as graffiti, peer pressure, tattoos, the impact of gang membership on family members, gangs and drugs, and other opportunities and alternatives for youth.

BOX 6.3
Continued

The program, which is now in its 7th year, has served over 3,000 youths. Evaluation has indicated that the number of individuals who have decided to join a gang has been significantly reduced. At pretest, 50% of the respondents indicated that they were undecided about joining a gang; following the program 90% of the respondents indicated that they had decided not to join a gang. A separate study indicated that, based on a random sample of the original program participants, 98% had not joined a gang. Four years after the program, a full 80% of students indicated that they thought that the program had helped them stay out of gangs, and 10% indicated that it had helped them not to use drugs (Wilson-Brewer, 1991).

Skills: Moving From
Contemplation to Preparation

BOX 6.4
"Having heard safe sex and various other prevention messages since grade school, by the time they reach their teens, they appear to have a fairly clear idea of which behaviors are safe or appropriate and of what they should and should not be doing. Nonetheless, statistics indicate that when the opportunity presents itself, these inhibitory messages give way to other interests" (Gibbons et al., 1995, p. 107).

As suggested by Prochaska's model of change, education alone is unlikely to bring about significant behavioral change. Although education may stimulate the move from precontemplation to contemplation, an individual must also progress through the preparation stage to the action stage for behavioral change to occur. This is where new skills become especially valuable. In skills-based programs, individuals are taught new behaviors and are encouraged to practice them and share their progress with others. Skills-based approaches that are generally well-suited to bring about change typically involve basic skills instruction, which often is facilitated through the use of role-playing and rehearsal that involves positive role models and careful feedback.

Skills for Adolescent Mental Health

Skills-based interventions often begin with the presentation of the particular skill to be taught. A tried-and-true method for presenting the new skill involves four steps: instruction in the nature and purpose of learning the skill, modeling the desired skill appropriately, rehearsing the skill with others, and receiving constructive feedback and positive reinforcement. For example, to teach assertive, positive communication style, the participants are shown the difference between an assertive and nonassertive response, followed by discussion and modeling of assertiveness.

The Youth Relationships Project, for example, uses a three-chair exercise to teach assertiveness. Three chairs are arranged so that two empty chairs (representing parents) are facing the other chair (representing the teen). One of the facilitators plays the role of a teen who is trying to make a request of her parents. The skit is repeated three times, to demonstrate how the request can be made passively, aggressively, or assertively. Following the demonstration a group discussion is held, during which the characteristic verbal and nonverbal features of passive, aggressive, and assertive communication are outlined. Facilitators then present a set of key phrases that can be used to direct an assertive request. To practice making assertive requests, teens are given typical situations and are encouraged to give each other feedback on their effort to use the phases they were taught. To provide ample opportunity for positive feedback and reinforcement, teens are asked to practice assertive requests before the next group meeting, where they receive feedback and further assistance as required.

Compas (1993) outlines a theory for skill development that is commensurate with a health-promotion strategy and the principles of prevention. Rather than focusing on skill deficits or deficiencies, this approach highlights the many ways that adolescents can acquire the basic strengths deemed necessary for positive mental health. Much of this work was informed by individuals who "defied the odds" and succeeded in their life choices, despite backgrounds of poverty, violence, and social deprivation. Based on these resilient individuals, Compas identified that *adolescent mental health* requires the development of skills to protect oneself from stress, and the development of skills to involve oneself in personally meaningful activities. Several of the identified skills that are valuable for advancing adolescent mental health include (Compas, 1993):

a. *Enhancing self-concept or self-esteem:* The purpose of this skill is to foster a positive feeling toward oneself, and a sense of self-efficacy and control. Often this involves exposing individuals to positive role models, developing cultural identity and pride, and teaching self-respect.

b. *Assertiveness skills:* Learning to behave assertively often involves the ability to express positive and negative feelings, to initiate, continue, and terminate general conversations, and to set limits for oneself. Assertiveness training also addresses nonverbal skills such as tone of voice, fluency of spoken words, facial expression, body expression, interpersonal distance, and eye contact.

c. *Social competence:* The development of mutually beneficial relations with others involves many interrelated abilities, such as the ability to resolve conflicts nonviolently, the ability to enter a group and form friendships, and the ability to negotiate with adults. Social competence and skills are a critical component of healthy functioning, especially in high-risk settings. One of the most consistent findings in the resilience literature, for example, is that children who are succeeding despite the odds have exceptionally strong social competence.

d. *Resistance and refusal training:* Resistance skills include the ability to identify and label social influences and pressure situations and the ability to resist the influence of peers. In combination with assertiveness and social competence, these skills serve to protect the individual from undue risk taking and susceptibility to negative influence.

e. *Problem solving and decision making:* Problem solving and decision making are components of most treatment and prevention programs. Problem solving is generally taught in five interrelated steps: defining the problem, examining variables and considering alternatives, isolating a plan, performing action steps, and evaluating the effects. Effective problem solvers have the ability to evaluate a number of different solutions to a problem, to use strategies with flexibility, and to learn from their mistakes.

f. *Self-management and self-control:* Self-assessment, self-monitoring, and self-reinforcement skills are all components of self-management. For someone to be an effective problem solver and to achieve one's desired goals, self-guidance is critical. Although many of the previous skills are necessary prerequisites, self-management must be attained for an individual to be free to choose his or her own goals and meet them successfully. This is a more advanced skill, which often comes from exposure to positive role models and environments as well as concerted efforts to acquire desired goals.

The application of these new skills can proceed in a number of ways, especially involving actual life circumstances as much as possible. One way to encourage individuals to apply the skills is to incorporate role plays into program content routinely. The inclusion of role play significantly increases the effectiveness of prevention efforts, by providing opportunities to rehearse skills and receive effective feedback (Blumberg, Chadwick, Fogarty, Speth, & Chadwick, 1991). Whereas behaviors that are not emotionally charged can be handled on an abstract level, "hot" topics (such as anger and refusal skills) need to include experiential components as much as possible.

BOX 6.5

Skills-Based Prevention: An Example Program

A time-honored method for preventing conflict has recently gained new popularity and application with peer-based interventions. In response to escalating violence, some schools are offering courses in mediation and conflict resolution strategies. Mediation generally involves 15-20 hours of training for teachers and students in helping people develop impulse control, communication skills, problem solving, and anger management. Students are then given the responsibility for mediating conflicts that occur among their peers while at school.

Results of these programs are generally positive. For example, during the first 2 years of the program at one Maui school in Hawaii, the number of fights dropped from 83 to 19. In a New York school, a program titled Resolving Conflict Creatively resulted in less name calling, physical violence, and fewer verbal put-downs in the classroom. In addition, students who had completed the program showed increased willingness to cooperate. Across programs, students reported that they have used the knowledge they gained in these programs both within and outside of the school setting (Wilson-Brewer, 1991, pp. 36-39).

Action:
Moving From Preparation to Action

BOX 6.6

"So often we talk about 'alienated' youth and our response is to 'rehabilitate.' Rehabilitation is not the opposite of alienation. Inclusion and engagement are the opposites of alienation" (Calhoun, 1992, p. 339).

Using action-based approaches for prevention is a relatively new method for social sciences, especially psychology. Action approaches involve encouraging and working with youth to integrate behavior changes into their everyday behavioral repertoire. According to Prochaska et al.'s (1992) model of change, making this step from preparation to action and maintenance is essential for prevention to have long-term effects. In most programs, however, it is assumed that lessons taught in the program will automatically be transferred to potentially problematic settings. Such transfer does not necessarily occur. As addiction researchers have long recognized, old settings often mean old behaviors. The same holds true for many other forms of behavior change as well. For most people, changes in behavior must be integrated into their lives and supported by accompanying changes in setting, peer group, and expectations of significant others.

Many of these important collateral changes can be promoted through the use of *social action* activities, which centralize the energy and focus of youth onto important issues in their communities, peer groups, schools, or all of these. Because youths prefer active involvement to passive instruction, this approach is particularly well-suited to their needs and creative energy. Social action signifies involvement and ownership, and encourages youths to find their own solutions to issues of personal concern, rather than being told what is important and how to proceed. Instead of focusing on their own problems, moreover, social action strives to enhance self-competence while assisting others. Thus, this action strategy capitalizes on the gains in maturity, motivation, and commitment that often flow from the strength of the group process, and allows participants to become empowered by sharing their knowledge and resources with others. Several promising social action approaches that follow warrant attention.

Casting At-Risk Individuals
in a "Helping Role"

A powerful approach to action-based prevention involves members of a target group in socially meaningful activities, such a volunteer work with troubled children, at sexual assault centers, or in geriatric facilities. Interestingly, the use of this approach, which

Riessman (1965) labeled the "helper-therapy principle" many years ago, has always been of interest to community mental health researchers and support groups, although the methods have seldom been in the foreground of behavior change research strategies.

Building on this philosophy, Kahn and Fua (1992) treated Aboriginal alcoholics by training them to become therapists for their communities. Trainees ($N = 240$) for the program were chosen on the recommendation of community leaders. Of those who were originally accepted, approximately 90% had a past and recent history of very severe alcohol abuse. Trainees were given an opportunity to discuss the effect of alcohol on their communities and were taught ways to help their community recover. A total of 60% completed the 2-year program, and over 95% of completers maintained their sobriety by the end of this period, which is well above the rate for most alcoholic treatment programs. In a related fashion, 80% of graduates are employed, with a majority of them working in fields related to alcohol treatment. These results suggest that casting individuals in the role of helpers may be an effective method both for treating known problems and for preventing the development of problems.

Expecting Responsible Action

Another creative method for applying the principles of social action involves the provision of responsibility. As stated by Calhoun (1992), "by demanding reciprocity, we imply that even the most difficult and wounded of them have something of worth that the larger society needs. By making demands, we acknowledge worth" (p. 337). This strategy challenges many of the well-entrenched methods of service delivery that are based on a deficit paradigm, in which recipients are provided with training and services that are decided primarily by others. Such a "passive" approach to assistance may foster dependency and lowers self-worth (Thompson, 1995). For example, family members who receive in-home support services from their community (e.g., childcare, medical information, crime prevention) report considerably more satisfaction and benefit when they are allowed to reciprocate and give something back. Instead of being cast in the role of someone who is dependent or helpless, individuals prefer to be seen for what they have to offer and to be given opportunities to demonstrate their value.

Teens as Community Resources, Inc. (TCR; Langstaff, 1991), which is largely youth organized and supervised, offers a strong example of this approach. The program provides small grants and technical assistance to youth-initiated community service and advocacy efforts. With the financial and technical assistance of TCR, teens in Boston have organized, among other things, a project to fix up a local youth center to be used for organizing conflict resolution workshops, neighborhood cleanups, police-teen dialogues and recreational activities, a youth fair to educate their peers on a number of issues concerning sexuality, and holiday meals for women staying at Boston City Hospital. The value of this program is expressed in the words of one of the participants: "I felt like people respected me. It feels good when anybody respects you. It's almost as though being treated more respectfully, you begin to see yourself more that way and act more that way" (p. 43).

Encouraging Continued
Growth and Change

Organizing teens to become involved in social action activities provides them with strong encouragement to use their newly gained skills, and it reinforces positive changes in attitudes about themselves and their communities. In a volunteer setting, adaptive skills are modeled by adults, reinforced by participants and coworkers, and further developed in staff training efforts. Researchers (e.g., Allen, Philliber, & Hoggson, 1990; Zimmerman & Rappaport, 1988) suggest that volunteer activities have the potential to promote the following opportunities for youth:

- Explore career roles
- Develop employment-related skills
- Make a contribution to their community
- Develop feelings of engagement and commitment
- Develop valuable connections with extra-familial adults
- Empower individuals to make personal and social changes
- Model socially appropriate behavior and see it modeled by others
- Be exposed to positive role models

- Gain adult recognition and respect
- Develop positive attitudes

These opportunities are critically needed by at-risk populations in general. In today's society it is often true that opportunities for success are very narrow in scope, such as through academic and athletic achievements. Involving high-risk individuals in community activities expands their opportunities for education, skill development, empowerment, and success.

BOX 6.7
Using Action-Based Prevention: An Example Program

The Teen Outreach Program (Allen et al., 1990) is a school-based program aimed at preventing teenage pregnancy and dropout by encouraging young people to perform volunteer service in their communities. Students are identified by teachers and guidance counselors as being at risk for dropout or pregnancy, and they participate in weekly classroom discussions of issues such as understanding yourself and values, communication skills, dealing with family stress, human growth and development, and issues related to parenting. This program is noteworthy for its insistence that the involved teens participate in a range of volunteer activities for a minimum of one-half hour per week. Subsequently, these activities are discussed and evaluated in the classroom.

The results of this study are illuminating in their prescriptions for future programs that plan to incorporate volunteer services. In the 4 years that this program has been evaluated, it has reduced teen pregnancy and school failure and dropout rates by approximately 30% to 50% relative to matched controls. Greater success is associated with a more intense volunteer component. After controlling for entry problem behaviors, students in programs that involved more volunteer work had fewer problems at the end of the evaluation period. Although students' gender, minority status, parents' years of education, or parent marriage status did not systematically influence outcome, evaluation indicated that age mediated outcome, with older students benefiting more than younger students.

Summary and Conclusions

In their review of risk prevention programs with adolescents, Fisher and Fisher (1992) conclude that modifying "risk behaviors" is best achieved by attending simultaneously to participants' needs for accurate information, motivational influences, and behavioral skills. In addition, recent prevention programs are starting to make use of community-based action-oriented strategies of prevention, with some degree of success. As suggested by Prochaska et al.'s (1992) model of change, preventative education, skills, and action are all needed to ensure long-term changes in behavior. When possible, programs should provide the opportunity for individuals to progress through all the stages of change. When this is not possible, program organizers should be aware of the need to consider what stage of change is current.

Despite large variations in types of changes, motivations for change, and methods for promoting change, the ways that people actually go about accomplishing their desired changes have been described in five primary steps: precontemplation, contemplation, preparation, action, and maintenance. Significantly, people most often cycle through these stages many times before they successfully add or eliminate a behavior from their repertoire. Therefore, change is best described as a cyclic process, as opposed to a circular one, because with each repetition comes new knowledge and experience that increases the potential of future success.

The education, skills, and action-based prevention strategies reviewed above all help individuals move from one stage of change to another. Education prompts the move from precontemplation, new skills prompt the move from contemplation to preparation, and action helps individuals move from preparation into social action and maintenance. Because there are many considerations to be made to match each situation, the choice of education, skills, and action methods should be decided with reference to the aims of the particular prevention program, the facilitators, the community need, and the relative effectiveness of each method for the specified clientele.

The contents of an individual prevention program should also be determined, in part, by the stage of change of the majority of the individuals in the program. Although it would be ideal for every program to encourage individuals to move through all of the steps of change, not all programs have the resources or time to provide this opportunity. In this case, program organizers may wish to encourage progress through only one stage of change, with the knowledge that further movement increases an individual's potential for change.

It is also important to recognize the current limitations to behavior change conceptualizations and technology. Earlier, we raised the issue of the most appropriate "level" of prevention; that is, is the community an appropriate target, or should we try to prevent violence within the context of the neighborhood, family, peer group, or individual? The response to this question appears to be that prevention needs to be integrated into all of these areas. On one hand, the complexity of the problem of violence, in particular, requires efforts that are integrative and comprehensive in design. Yet, on the other hand, comprehensiveness itself may not be a "magic bullet"; any individual prevention program can be successful at addressing a small but important number of these concerns (Dryfoos, 1991).

CHAPTER SEVEN

The Youth Relationships Project

BOX 7.1

"Families are failing to tell kids how to build strong relationships and live principled lives. As a result, many young people have lost touch with what really constitutes a healthy relationship. The Youth Relationships Project is designed to dispel gender myths and promote egalitarian relationships among high-risk youth. It is a practical way of preventing a cycle of abuse from developing" (Wolfe, cited in B. Murray, 1995, p. 48).

This final chapter is devoted to discussing the structure of the Youth Relationships Project (YRP). The YRP was developed as a way to help youth understand the abuse of power and control in their own relationships. By offering youth opportunities to explore the richness and rewards of relationships, they become more eager to learn about choices and responsibilities. The "initiation phase" of social dating is a prime opportunity to become aware of the ways in which violent and abusive behavior toward intimate partners may occur, often without purpose or intention. This premise holds true not only for individuals from violent and abusive family backgrounds where negative experiences were prominent, but it applies to other adolescents as well.

Instead of approaching the topic of relationship violence as if it were a plague or a blight that affects only "disturbed" individuals, important messages about healthy relationships can be comfortably interwoven into the common interests and concerns of all youth. Early adolescence is an opportune time to consider all of the subtle, as well as the overt, forms of inequality, violence, discrimination, and abuse that can operate almost silently in the background of peer and dating relationships. Making the effort to discover one's own prejudices, stereotypes, gender-based beliefs, and similar expectations of dating partners is a worthy investment in learning to develop egalitarian relationships.

Engaging youth in creating their own visions of healthy, nonviolent relationships as early as possible has one other potential benefit. Regardless of their own personal level of risk, we may succeed in downplaying the status and glorification of "violence" that so often occupies the interest of adolescents, and instead place more emphasis on personal choices and responsibility.

Benefiting from the tremendous gains in prevention activities that have focused predominantly on health-related behaviors, an early intervention/prevention model was formulated in the previous chapter in relation to various stages of behavioral change and the methods that are most likely to be successful with youth. Again, a major theme that emerges in this model is the importance of gender dynamics, which we define as power in relationships as well as attitudes and values regarding gender roles, similar to Amaro (1995). Understanding the importance of gender issues is a crucial factor in the formation of this prevention model.

Our approach relies heavily on the strength of empowerment in the context of adolescent development and social dating. As noted previously, empowerment involves "personal power" that is built through personal connections with others, which in turn creates the freedom to be open and receptive with others. The evolving health promotion viewpoint of violence prevention fits very well with this feminist viewpoint of empowerment. The principles of participatory education, in particular, have been well adapted to health education and disease prevention.

Empowerment and health promotion methods differ in important ways from more traditional health education/intervention approaches, such as public awareness campaigns (e.g., "don't drink and drive") or public health initiatives (e.g., flu shots). Health education and intervention strategies have been generally passive by design, perhaps to reach the largest possible audience by blanketing everyone with a simple message or action to follow. Moreover, these approaches assume (based on their paradigm) that individuals benefit most by being the recipient of actions designed by others.

In contrast, education programs designed to promote social change and individual or group empowerment are more active by nature. These strategies, which are often aimed at promoting determinants of psychological as well as physical health and well-being, assume that people achieve control over their lives through their own efforts and critical thinking. Such control, in turn, assists them in recognizing some of the underlying determinants of their dissatisfaction or problems, describing alternatives, and taking action that leads to changes in their personal situation as well as society. Thus, empowerment strategies, by design, encourage people *to act on the system,* rather than *to be acted on by the system* (Wallerstein, 1992).

History and Development of the Youth Relationships Project

In 1989, the Institute for the Prevention of Child Abuse in Toronto, Ontario hosted a conference to discuss expert opinion as to the "best ways" to prevent *child abuse.* This organization was dedicated to finding more proactive ways to eliminate the significant problems arising from child abuse, and recognized the importance of working with families to reduce the likelihood of abuse well before common problems became insurmountable.

Given the prominent similarities in the backgrounds, personalities, and behavioral expression of known offenders against women and children, we embarked on a search to understand more about the processes involved along the way in the formation of violent attitudes and behavior. We found that many children and adults who had experienced violence had to overcome significant injuries to both their physical and psychological makeup. We also found that, in some cases, these injuries lasted a lifetime. Along with many other researchers and clinicians, we were struck by the observation that many offenders seemed be repeating a pattern of behavior that was very similar to what they had experienced. For example, Oliver (1993) concluded on the basis of a substantive review that one third of those children who experienced abuse developed a pattern of seriously inept, neglectful, or abusive parenting styles; another one third were at risk for developing dysfunctional parenting strategies. Kaufman and Zigler (1987) similarly concluded that 30% ± 5% of abused children become abusive adults.

We presumed that these intergenerational patterns could be influenced through a concerted effort to inform youth (mostly young men) of the abuses of power and control and provide them with more understanding and skill at nonviolent forms of communication. Similarly, we presumed that young women, whether they had been the direct victims of abusive relationships or not, could benefit from greater knowledge of self-awareness, self-protection, and intolerance for sexual and physical forms of harassment and abuse, coupled with greater skill at self-assertion and effective communication.

Based on the emerging literature pertaining to the development of violent behavior and abusive relationships, a curriculum aimed at preventing violence in youth relationships was constructed. As emphasized throughout this book, it was our view that midadolescence offered a valuable window of opportunity—a period of development that could alter the course of current and future relationship development. Although adolescence is not as significant as early periods of development (i.e., infancy and early childhood; Sroufe & Fleeson, 1986) in terms of setting the stage for relationship formation, it was our view that the formation of social dating relationships required many adaptational skills that were similar in kind to those required of the younger child (such as a sense of security, trust, reciprocation, and so on).

Ostensibly, knowledge gained and skills learned during midadolescence would transfer readily to the youths' subsequent relationships with their marital partners and with their children. Whether or not a psychoeducational program could compensate to a significant degree for a lack of positive caregivers during childhood (and overcome the powerful developmental trajectory that is often cast by maltreatment) is clearly a question that must be answered empirically. The cost of waiting for major problems to be detected later on, when even less can be done to reverse the process, provides a strong motivation for such an attempt.

Founding Philosophy

> **BOX 7.2**
> At the Youth Relationships Project, we needed to find ways to work *with* youth to assist them in making choices, and learning skills for nonviolent means of communication with their current and future partners.

From its beginnings in 1991, the Youth Relationships Project has been organized around the principles of prevention discussed in Chapter 4: to allow people to have choice and voice, trust and responsibility, respect and recognition, and to empower them to make positive life changes. We needed to consider what these principles meant for a project geared toward youth who have experienced various forms of maltreatment and who were at risk for repeating the pattern of abuse in their own relationships.

First, we acknowledged that youth in our society are often disenfranchised, due to the real gap between mainstream opportunities and their own realistic choices. For example, they are lured by the adult world and encouraged to take on "adult responsibilities," but are seldom awarded the privileges associated with these responsibilities. This distinction translates into youth being in a nonpower position when it comes to issues of major significance to their lives. In many instances such age-based limitation of freedom and responsibility is both necessary and understandable (such as driving, use of alcohol, educational requirements, and so on). Because of the transitional nature of their "permissible" activities and limitations, however, it comes as little surprise that many youths lack conviction for establishing the leadership or fostering opportunities to advance many other issues of importance primarily to themselves.

We also needed to acknowledge that most of the youth who we wish to enfranchise have been coping with more than their share of problems for some time. Many of them have been bouncing in and out of social service agencies for many years, and many are in the official care of the state or province. In some cases the most consistent and stable person in the lives of these teens has been their social worker, although they may have known one another only a few years at most. In an attempt to develop a reasonable service plan that compensates in part for their family-based problems, these youths may have received sporadic treatment services, often in connection with some aspect of their behavior that drew (negative) attention (e.g., stealing, problems at school, peer rejection). Unfortunately such well-intended services, delivered in a problem-focused, reactive manner, often leave the individual with little understanding of their strengths and uniqueness and instead can limit his or her self-efficacy (Kazdin, 1993). In response, we chose to emphasize the importance of a competency-based program designed to *build strengths*, rather than a treatment effort designed to identify and eliminate weaknesses.

With these things in mind, we decided that a program that purports to empower vulnerable youth needed to be grounded in the philosophy that each youth has a prominent say in how the program operates and what information it conveys. Accordingly, the YRP has sought ways to work *with* youth to assist them in forming choices and in learning nonviolent means of communicating with their current and future partners. Significantly, youths' responsibility and power in the group could not be an illusion or a gimmick; participants must have ownership of their program and a say in what goes on within the 2 hours each week that they meet.

Organizing Principles

BOX 7.3
Selected written responses to the question: "What I liked best about the group was"

   Talking to others and realizing they have the same
      feelings as I do
   Open discussion, group agreement, and the relaxing
      atmosphere
   The way we talked and discussed issues
   Hearing different views on certain situations
   The attempt at making everyone feel involved in group
      discussion
   Talking about real life experiences

Putting our philosophy and principles into action has been a challenging process that we regard as ongoing rather than definitive or complete. With the understanding that there is a universe of possibilities for promoting healthy relationships among youth, we outline below five of the most prominent ways we have chosen to put the philosophies of prevention into practice.

Encouraging Youth Input
and Responsibility

It is particularly important that ownership of each group's structure and activities resides in the hands of the participants, not the facilitators. Accordingly, one of the requirements for cofacilitators is a willingness to give up the power that they are accorded due to their age and their leadership position, and to relate to participants as equals. This requirement is not always easy to realize, especially if a facilitator serves in some other role with one of the participants (such as a teacher or social worker). For this reason, we recommend that facilitators of YRP groups be someone who is unfamiliar to all participants and who does not have a role conflict (see Wolfe et al., 1996).

In addition, teens are given the responsibility of drawing up a group agreement during the first session. This agreement sets down group rules for the remainder of the sessions, and it is both generated and enforced by the youth themselves. Young people quickly identify the importance of confidentially and mutual respect. Additionally, they often set and agree to respect rules requiring regular attendance and the avoidance of drugs or alcohol prior to meetings.

Youths clearly benefit from having a sense of ownership of the group. In our regular postevaluations of the program completed by participants, reference is often made to the value of the group agreement (e.g., one teen stated that she "could talk openly because we had a group agreement"). Other participants have reflected on the value of mutual respect, commenting that "people were supportive of your opinion and you weren't laughed at," and that during group you could "talk about anything and not worry about people putting you down." As these statements illustrate, giving youth input and responsibility is a strong first step toward gaining their trust, respect, and their willingness to work with each other and with the cofacilitators to promote healthy, nonviolent relationships.

Providing Positive Role Models

Strategies to end violence must confront not only abuse in individual relationships, but the attitudes and systemic structures within social institutions that glorify and perpetuate the problem. To empower young people to make personal choices that do not abuse power, it was first necessary to examine our own power and privilege (e.g. white, adult, facilitator), and be aware of how we may abuse this power unintentionally. In this regard, we instruct cofacilitators on ways to model power sharing and equal relationships consistently. This (somewhat uncommon) exposure to positive role models is a powerful mechanism in itself for promoting change among vulnerable youth. To encourage the process, cofacilitators are required after each session to rate and describe the extent to which they felt they were effective models of egalitarian relationships.

Another method for providing positive role models involves exposure to others who have accomplished some of the objectives that participants are currently facing. We approach this issue in two ways. First, we invite former participants to return as "youth cofacilitators" to lead discussions and share experiences on occasion, which demonstrates how the program has been put to use. To provide models of mastery, we also organize one session in which people from formerly abusive relationships are invited to speak. These speakers (usually one man who has been abusive and one woman who was abused) have been carefully interviewed by project members prior to attendance to ensure their sincerity and understanding of the program, and they are usually well-known in the local community for their outreach efforts. Hearing firsthand from these adults (who in many ways have faced and overcome problems similar to those of the youths' parents) is often described by participants as a powerful and extremely helpful experience.

Peer Group Discussion

In a review of the characteristics of successful programs with youth, Dryfoos (1991) and Greene (1993) both concluded that an important characteristic of successful programs was the opportunity for open discussion among group members. Similarly, we chose to give priority to group discussion over other presentation formats in general because of the perceived value of this "naturalistic" mode of expression and learning. As any teacher can attest, young people often prefer to discuss provocative or stimulating information among themselves rather than in a passive or receptive manner alone, which may serve to clarify, translate, and evaluate its personal significance.

BOX 7.4
Angie and Josh's Story

Over the course of the weekly meetings youths typically develop a strong bond that provides a supportive environment and a safe container for them. Often they will discuss relationship difficulties with each other outside of the actual group setting (i.e., typically before and after sessions and on the break). We (the cofacilitators) came to learn about one occasion when one of the young women in the group was encouraged by a young man not to meet her abusive boyfriend following the session, as was her plan. Instead, they went to a nearby coffee shop to discuss her relationship. The young man expressed his concerns about her relationship and made clear his willingness to support her in any way that he could.

Peer group discussion is a powerful vehicle for giving young persons a voice. Formatting information around peer discussion gives participants the sense that they have something valuable to contribute. Peer group discussion also facilitates mutual connection, support, and understanding, and thereby opposes the common feelings of being alone with one's problems. As many teens have commented, one of the most valuable aspects of this group can be having the chance "to learn that there are other people with maybe the same problems."

Focus on Strengths

Although focusing on strengths sounds straightforward, this is not always the case. Antiviolence educational materials, especially those that are treatment focused, often emphasize the "identified problem" and teach *what not to do*, which is an easy and understandable trap to fall into. Because of well-entrenched paradigms and limited funding, service providers often focus their time and energy on changing unhealthy patterns, to the exclusion of developing healthy ones.

Throughout the YRP curriculum we have attempted to strike more of a balance between the prevention of undesirable (i.e., violent, abusive) behavior patterns or relationships and the promotion of desirable communication and problem-solving skills (for example). An old adage of behavior modification still rings true: If you want to maintain a reduction in a problem behavior (such as aggression) you need to make a corresponding effort to develop a desirable replacement (such as assertion). Prevention, after all, means more that stopping something bad—it should also offer something positive and of lasting value!

Provide Youth With Resources to Get Help

Finally, we live up to the ideals of prevention by empowering youth with the knowledge and skills to recognize early signs of an abusive relationship, when and how to get help, and how to be of assistance to others. Participants often indicate that learning how to avoid violence in their own relationships is of particular and immediate value to them (for example, "learning ways to stay out of violent relationships," and "realizing the signs of violence"). During group, youths learn to recognize the warning signals of a potentially violent relationship. They also explore the pattern and cycle of violence in relationships, and learn about the different ways that the cycle of violence can become self-perpetuating.

Sometimes a problem situation can be avoided or resolved simply through appropriate and informed use of existing resources, rather than the provision of something unique or specialized alone. Learning to access such resources without triggering an alarmist reaction or becoming frustrated, however, requires some experience and awareness. In this regard, participants are taught concrete methods for obtaining help and advice from their peers and their communities without sending out signals that might trigger a "crisis management" response by the very systems from which they sought assistance (for example, "to whom do you turn for help if you care about your partner but believe he is becoming more and more abusive?"). Youths are encouraged to explore the range of social services available to them, and they practice phoning or visiting various agencies with simulated problems (each agency is first informed by a facilitator of the true purpose of the call and has given consent to participate in the exercise).

In summary, we intended that the organization of the YRP would reflect the importance of youth input and responsibility, positive role models, peer group discussion, an appreciation of individual strengths, and the realistic appraisal of resources and how to access them. From this core we established several intervention goals and educational objectives (based on our developmental model) that brought these organizing principles to life. Although a description of the specific exercises and curricula is beyond the scope of this volume, we present an overview of the framework of our intervention model and corresponding program content. Readers who are interested in the specific *delivery* of the YRP curriculum are referred to the *Youth Relationships Manual* (Wolfe et al., 1996) for full description of the weekly sessions, exercises, and related intervention procedures.

The YRP Intervention Model: Moving Theory Into Practice

Defining Intervention Goals

What are the early stages of relationship dynamics that are most likely to lead to future violence or abuse? By midadolescence, many youth engage in so many unfamiliar and risk-taking activities that such behaviors are usually considered either normal, harmless, or impossible to bypass or influence. Some adolescents who are not yet involved in compromising risk behaviors (those who are younger, primarily) may be at risk of *initiating or becoming involved* in health compromising behaviors. In terms of relationship violence, therefore, we have shown that early- to midadolescence is an important time in the formation of intimate relationships and, consequently, it is when the beginning stages of the abuse of power and control may be more easily reversible or avoided.

Using our theoretical model from Chapter 5 as a guide, the first step in the formation of the YRP was to identify aspects of relationship dynamics that are suitable targets for prevention and promotion. Then, several critical choices had to be made to make the theoretical model "workable." Because our model of relationship dysfunction considers historical and current risk factors that cut across broad levels (i.e., cultural, familial, individual) and psychological domains (i.e., cognitive/affective, behavioral, interpersonal), we needed to distill those constructs that we felt were "current operatives" for interpersonal risk. That is, what factors may be currently operating on the formation of healthy versus high-risk relationships among younger adolescents, and how might we promote desired outcomes?

Rather than attempting to address historical factors directly (such as negative childhood experiences), this strategy focuses on building on current strengths and exposing youths to healthy role models at a point in time when they are motivated to learn. In addition, although some level of abusive or violent behavior may be emergent in this population of youth, we assumed that no pattern or violent dynamic has been established as yet. Thus, our goal was to *prevent* violence in close relationships and to *promote* positive, egalitarian relationships.

We identified several current risk factors that are likely to have a strong influence on the formation of abusive relationships. Our intervention concerns were then formulated in response to these primary risk factors, as summarized in Table 7.1 (the corresponding curricula for these objectives is discussed in a subsequent section).

Establishing a "Fit" Between Services and Recipients

A second critical choice was to identify the most suitable subpopulation of youth, which again flowed directly from our theoretical model. Salient historical variables were previously identified as clear "risk markers" for interpersonal violence, with child maltreatment being the most empirically supported. We decided that any youth with a history of maltreatment could be considered at risk of relationship problems and could, therefore, benefit from our pro-

TABLE 7.1. Moving From Theory to Practice—The Youth Relationships
Project's (YRP) Intervention Model

YRP prevention goals

1. To prevent violence in close relationships (peer, dating) with respect to both
"offender" and "victim" behaviors

2. To promote positive, egalitarian relationships

YRP target population

Risk status: History of child maltreatment, including one or more of the following
experiences: (a) witnessing domestic violence; (b) physical abuse; (c)
sexual abuse; (d) emotional abuse; (e) physical or emotional neglect

YRP intervention concerns

Cognitive/affective dimension	*Current risk factors*
I. Victim/victimizer relationship models	— Current insecure attachment models — High interpersonal sensitivity/hostility
II. Power-abusive relationship views and values	— Gender-role rigidity — Sexist, proviolent relationship expectations
Behavioral dimension	
III. Conflict resolution and communication skills	— High power assertion in relationships — High conflict avoidance — Limited problem-solving ability — Low positive verbal assertion in relationships — High risk taking/low safety and protection skills

---

gram. In addition to youths receiving child welfare or protective
services, this criteria could be readily expanded to involve a much
larger population of children and adolescents. For example, the
common use of physical punishment may also be a reasonable risk
marker for relationship dysfunction (Straus & Kantor, 1994), although this approach would fit more appropriately into a broader-
based, primary prevention strategy.

One issue we kept in mind in relation to identifying our target
group was the possibility of stigma being attached to the program,
such as would occur if the program was seen as a form of "treatment" rather than prevention. An unwritten tenet of youth subculture is that it is better to be "bad" than "mad," with youth being
suspicious and generally reticent of adult-initiated treatment. Moving

to a more universal application of a prevention program, such as employing high school populations, is one way to avoid such stigma. When behavior change methods covering several interwoven psychological "components" (such as high interpersonal sensitivity, gender-role rigidity, and limited problem-solving ability), however, are applied to too large of a sample at once, they are often capable of addressing only the basic issues and consequently fail to meet the specific needs of high-risk participants (Dryfoos, 1991).

A practical strategy, and one that the YRP has used successfully, is to advertise the program clearly as a health promotion opportunity rather than treatment. The emphasis is placed on knowledge and skills that are of primary interest to participants (in our case, social dating, conflict resolution, and communication), and which also have no "ceiling" or upper limit (i.e., relationships). Thus, individuals have a choice to participate or not, and have a say in what they will be learning and applying.

The manner in which the personal needs and situational opportunities can be matched for the benefit of individual youths was demonstrated by Sanderson and Cantor (1995) in their study of social dating skills. They discovered that education methods that emphasized interpersonal communication are a good match for those individuals with predominantly intimacy goals in social dating, whereas education that focuses on technical skills was more effective for those with predominantly identity goals. Notably, teens were less likely to engage in risky sexual behavior when they were involved in dating situations *that encouraged their own goal-relevant activities*. These different developmental needs inform us as to the best manner for educating youth concerning dating relationships and sexuality (for example).

Program Location and Setting

The location of a prevention program for youth bears an important relationship to its accessibility and ultimate success. Because of our model's emphasis on the broad cultural and societal contributors to the creation of a violent context for relationship development, we chose to adopt a community-based approach (rather than an agency- or school-based location). A community location favors the reciprocal involvement of youths and community agents/ resources both directly (e.g., community volunteers, intervention facilitators, intervention facility) and indirectly (e.g., through popular support, beneficiaries of program fund-raising, and so on).

The setting for working with youths must also ensure privacy and foster a sense of community and cooperative spirit. Ideally, such a setting would be far removed from the pressures of school, peer groups, family members, and adult supervisors, although such a setting is rarely available. We chose to conduct our groups at various community locations, depending on availability of private space and accessibility for participants. A comfortable "group room" atmosphere can be created within any setting that affords an opportunity for creativity, open discussion, and a sense of safety. In contrast, classrooms, activity rooms, or any space that creates distraction or is not conducive to discussion of personal topics would be unsuitable.

Program Content and Delivery

BOX 7.5

Sonja frequently spoke during sessions of difficulties in her relationship with her mother. Her mother abused alcohol, which often led to violent arguments between them. Sonja felt unable to make her mother understand the negative effect that her drinking had on both of their lives. After the session in which we taught assertive communication skills, Sonja asked if she could take the information handouts home with her so that she could remember what to do during arguments with her mother. Sonja began to apply this new skill to situations involving her mother, and found her ability to communicate assertively to be quite helpful in her relationship with her mother.

Specific Aims and Intervention Plans

Based on our understanding of change and our model of vulnerability, we designed a prevention program focusing on three specific

TABLE 7.2 The Youth Relationships Project (YRP): Matching Program
Content to Identified Risk Factors

Relationship Dimensions and Current Risk Factors	*Matching Program Content in YRP Sessions*
I. *Victim/victimizer relationship models*	*Titles of corresponding sessions:*

Current risk factors:
Insecure attachment models
High interpersonal sensitivity and
   hostility
	Knowledge and skills exercises:
	"Power in relationships"
	"Explosions and assertions"
	"Choosing partners and sex-role
	   stereotypes"
	Social action exercises:
	"Getting to know community
	   helpers for relationship violence"
	"Getting out and about in the
	   community: Social service
	   agencies"

II. *Power-abusive relationship views and values*	*Titles of corresponding sessions:*

Current risk factors:
Gender-role rigidity
Sexist, proviolent relationship
   expectations and attitudes
	Knowledge and skills exercises:
	"Defining relationship violence"
	"Gender socialization and societal
	   pressure"
	"Choosing partners and sex-role
	   stereotypes"
	"Sexism"
	"Media and sexism"
	Social action exercises:
	"Confronting sexism and violence
	   against women"

III. *Conflict resolution and communication skills*	*Titles of corresponding sessions:*

Current risk factors:
High power assertion
High conflict avoidance
Limited problem-solving ability
Low positive verbal assertion
High risk taking/low safety and
   protection skills
	Knowledge and skills exercises:
	"Defining powerful relationships:
	   Equality, empathy, and
	   emotional expressiveness"
	"Defining powerful relationships:
	   Assertiveness instead of
	   aggressiveness"
	"Date rape and learning how to
	   handle dating pressure"
	"Date rape: Being clear, being safe"
	
	Social action exercises:
	"Getting out and about in the
	   community: Social action to end
	   relationship violence"

aims. These aims defined the learning objectives for both the psychological (i.e., cognitive, affective, and behavioral) and the interpersonal growth of each participant, and incorporated information, skills, and social action learning components. To address these aims, we located or developed information and skills exercises to match the risk factors identified in our theoretical model (see Table 7.2).

Specific Aim 1: To Increase Cognitive Awareness and Understanding Among Male and Female Youths About Issues Related to Healthy Versus Unhealthy Relationships. Prevention targets related to this aim include understanding dating violence, woman abuse, and sexist attitudes and beliefs.

Youths begin the YRP program by discussing and debating issues related to healthy versus unhealthy relationships (e.g., dating violence, wife assault, proaggression attitudes and beliefs, conflict resolution skills, and building healthy relationships). Films of dating violence are presented, and teens discuss the impact and extent of personal violence. To increase interest and participation, for example, teens construct a collage of positive and negative images of men and women from magazines to explore the nature of male and female stereotypes. To impart accurate information, we provide youth with technical information concerning the prevalence of violence, the typical victims of violence, and the myths associated with violence in families and in relationships. Information about the effects of abuse are personalized by hearing men and women talk about their experiences in violent relationships.

Specific Aim 2: To Develop Skills to Help Adolescents Build Healthy Relationships, and to Recognize and Respond to Abuse in Their Own Relationships and in Relationships of Their Peers. Prevention targets include adaptive communication, safety skills, assertiveness, appropriate expression of feelings, and problem solving.

Youths need to observe how others handle conflict, arousal, or debate appropriately, without resorting to power-based solutions or ineffective forms of communication. A series of exercises dealing with communication and conflict resolution skills combines the educational strategies of discussion, modeling, and role play, and youths are taught to apply these skills to everyday experiences.

Specific Aim 3: To Consolidate Learning of New Attitudes and Skills and to Increase Competency Through Community Involvement and Social Action. This phase was designed to provide participants with information about resources in the community that can assist them in managing unfamiliar, stressful issues in their relationships, and to provide them with experiential opportunities involving community agents.

Young people benefit most from prevention programs that build in ample opportunity for their own personal commitment and action (in this case, to end violence against women). Accordingly, we developed community-based, hands-on experiences in which participants are given an opportunity to practice solving hypothetical problems by involving their peer and community resources. As pairs, they receive a hypothetical problem situation and go about finding ways in the community to receive help and advice. Cofacilitators act as consultants and make their approach to community persons as realistic, yet successful, as possible.

Finally, participants organize and carry out a community project or activity that involves a violence prevention theme (as illustrated in Box 7.6). Through social action, they reaffirm their personal and group commitment to end violence against women and have the opportunity to demonstrate this commitment to others. Group members have organized such events as walkathons, dances, face painting, and theatrical demonstrations to raise money for local agencies or groups that serve victims or perpetrators of abuse.

An overview of the sessions corresponding to the identified risk factors and specific aims is shown in Table 7.2. The manner in which these sessions are organized in the actual curriculum is shown in Table 7.3, based on the *Youth Relationships Manual* (Wolfe et al., 1996).

Future Directions

The program described in this book was established on the belief that the goal of preventing violence in relationships can be achieved

TABLE 7.3 The Youth Relationships Project (YRP): Program Sections
and Weekly Sessions[a]

Section I: *Violence in Close Relationships:*
              It's All About Power
Session   1—Introduction to group
Session   2—Power in relationships: Explosions and assertions
Session   3—Defining relationship violence: Power abuses

Section II: *Breaking the Cycle of Violence:*
               What We Can Choose to Do and What We Can Choose Not to Do
Session   4—Defining powerful relationships: Equality, empathy, and emotional
              expressiveness
Session   5—Defining power relationships: Assertiveness instead of aggressiveness
Session   6—Date rape: Being clear, being safe

Section III: *The Contexts of Relationship Violence*
Session   7—Date rape and learning how to handle dating pressure
Session   8—Gender socialization and societal pressure
Session   9—Choosing partners and sex-role stereotypes
Session 10—Sexism
Session 11—Media and sexism

Section IV: *Making a Difference:*
               Working Toward Breaking the Cycle of Violence
Session 12—Confronting sexism and violence against women
Session 13—Getting to know community helpers for relationship violence
Session 14—Getting out and about in the community: Social service agencies
Session 15—Getting out and about in the community: Social service agencies
Session 16—Getting out and about in the community: Social action to end
              relationship violence
Session 17—Getting out and about in the community: Social action to end
              relationship violence
Session 18—Celebration!

---

a. From the table of contents of the *Youth Relationships Project Manual* (Wolfe et al., 1996).

by maximizing youths' involvement and participation in promoting nonviolence. This strategy derives from a theoretical model relating early childhood maltreatment to the emergence of subsequent relationship violence, especially during mid to late adolescence. Because of the potential "domino effect" of abuse and neglect on developmental tasks, such children are at risk for becoming abusive

> **BOX 7.6**
> Aaron stood out in the first several sessions because of his extremely racist and sexist views. We were surprised to see him show up for each week because his views were so openly at odds with the mandate of the group. There was, however, a slow but steady evolution in Aaron's attitudes and by the last few sessions, he was the one we could rely on the most to carry through on homework assignments related to the fund-raiser event. He was a key player in the nonviolence march, which was held on one very cold winter day toward the group's end.

or violent, or being the victims of such treatment, in their formative intimate relationships.

Prevention research is at an early stage of development relative to the range of issues that are linked to violence against women. Thus, the success of the YRP will likely be challenged by unknown factors associated with working with youths who have backgrounds of abuse and neglect, and especially by the limitations of evaluating the prevention (in effect, the *nonoccurrence*) of private behaviors that emerge over several years. Notwithstanding these concerns, the YRP is one of the first systematic efforts aimed at interrupting the processes leading to relationship violence among persons who are at significant risk of showing such behavior, or being the victim of such behavior, in young adulthood. Importantly, the procedures for the intervention were carefully developed over several years of pilot efforts to ensure an adequate "match" between the needs and interests of this population and the content and methods of delivery.

Our theoretical model presumes that relationship violence begins with "initiation" behaviors prior to age 15 (e.g., teasing, pushing, throwing things), and escalates over the next several years of adolescence and young adulthood among those at risk. We have found support for this model on the basis of high school and child protective service (CPS) samples, indicating that both males and females engage in low-intensity coercion and abuse during midadolescence (Wolfe, Wekerle, Reitzel-Jaffe, & Lefebvre, in press). Furthermore, youths with maltreatment backgrounds are more likely than nonmaltreated peers to be more coercive and abusive toward a dating partner. Interested readers are referred to the studies by Wolfe et al. (in press) and Wekerle, Wolfe, and Lefebvre (1995).

The Next Steps

The developmental orientation underlying the YRP model and program implies somewhat of a departure from most current efforts to detect, treat, or punish youths who show signs of violence. First of all, educators can be more sensitive to the emergent efforts by vulnerable youth to learn how to behave in relationships without the benefit of prior healthy models or careful guidance. Educational and therapeutic interventions, accordingly, can be implemented to strengthen developmentally relevant tasks or skills. Equally important is the implication, based on this orientation, that prevention and intervention efforts can be planned from an earlier point in time in such a way that undesirable (and potentially problematic) behavior patterns can be minimized. Rather than relying solely on detection and punitive sanctions, a developmentally guided intervention/prevention strategy works on the principle of providing the least intrusive, earliest assistance possible. The focus is shifted away from identifying misdeeds of young persons and is directed more toward empowering them to become intolerant of oppression, discrimination, abuse, and violence and to seek to establish healthy, nonviolent relationships.

One key factor in the future success of prevention programs with youth is the recognition of the need of all young people for support and education about relationship issues and personal safety. Adequate supports, both instrumental and emotional, are important for the healthy functioning of adolescents. Such supportive services should include, at a minimum, agency-based services, quasi-formal supports (e.g., self-help groups), and informal supports that are accessible to individuals. The expansion of existing youth and family services to include more "at-risk" youth at an earlier point in time, however, remains a largely unexplored platform. The advantage of an empowerment strategy, in contrast to an interception approach, is that it provides a blend of services in a youth-centered format. Such a model, however, requires a different allocation of resources and professional commitment than is presently in place.

Finally, we should encourage diversity of styles and opportunities for the development of unique resources for children and youth. High-risk youth are extremely diverse in their needs and not all will "fit" into an educational or training program or welcome such assistance. These issues will require a new or expanded paradigm to approach the complexity of needs of this diverse population. Prevention efforts should not be limited only to identified "risk" populations or those who are currently faced with child-rearing responsibilities; we must encourage more awareness and flexibility of gender roles and responsibilities during childhood, adolescence, and young adulthood and strive to involve males more often in educational efforts (Wolfe, 1991). Researchers and practitioners have begun to approach such solutions by developing interesting materials and opportunities to engage young adults early on during the formation of their attitudes and behaviors toward intimate partners. We hope the intentions of this book and its related manual are achieved through meaningful contributions to these efforts.

References

Achenbach, T. M. (1982). *Developmental psychopathology* (2nd ed.). New York: John Wiley.

Ainsworth, M. D. S., Blehar, M. C., Waters, E., & Wall, S. (1978). *Patterns of attachment: A psychological study of the strange situation.* Hillsdale, NJ: Lawrence Erlbaum.

Albee, G. W. (1980). A competency model to replace the defect model. In M. Gibbs, J. Lachenmeyer, & J. Sigal (Eds.), *Community psychology: Theoretical and empirical approaches* (pp. 213-238). New York: Gardner.

Albee, G. (1985). The argument for primary prevention. *Journal of Primary Prevention,5,* 213-219.

Albee, G. W., Bond, L. A., & Monsey, T. V. C. (Eds.). (1992). *Improving children's lives: Global perspectives on prevention.* Newbury Park: Sage.

Allen, J. P., Philliber, S., & Hoggson, N. (1990). School-based prevention of teenage pregnancy and school dropout: Process evaluation of the national replication of the Teen Outreach Program. *American Journal of Community Psychology, 18*(4), 505-524.

Amaro, H. (1995). Love, sex, and power: Considering women's realities in HIV prevention. *American Psychologist, 50,* 437-447.

Anthony, J. A., & Reeves, M. C. (1989). *Children in foster families.* Chicago, IL: Lyceum.

Are school boards heading for a crisis? (1995, September 15). *The London Free Press,* p. A3.

Averill, J. R. (1983). Studies on anger and aggression: Implications for theories of emotion. *American Psychologist, 38,* 1145-1160.

Azar, B. (1995). Foster care has bleak history. *APA Monitor, 26,* 8.

Babcock, J. C., Waltz, J., Jacobson, N. S., & Gottman, J. M. (1993). Power and violence: The relation between communication patterns, power discrepancies, and domestic violence. *Journal of Consulting and Clinical Psychology, 61*(1), 40-50.

Baby, F., Chéné, J., & Dudas, H. (1992). *Les femmes dans les vidéoclip: Sexisme et violence.* Etude réalisé pour le Conseil de Statut de la Femme, Gouvernement de Québec.

Bakken, L., & Romig, C. (1992). Interpersonal needs in middle adolescents: Companionship, leadership, and intimacy. *Journal of Adolescence, 15*, 301-316.

Bandura, A. (1989). Human agency in social cognitive theory. *American Psychologist, 44*, 1175-1184.

Bangert-Drowns, R. L. (1988). The effects of school-based substance abuse education—a meta-analysis. *Journal of Education, 18*, 243-264.

Barongan, C., & Hall, G. C. N. (1995). The influence of misogynous rap music on sexual aggression against women. *Psychology of Women Quarterly, 19*, 195-207.

Barry, F. D. (1994). A neighborhood-based approach: What is it? In G. B. Melton & F. D. Barry (Eds.), *Protecting children from child abuse and neglect: Foundations for a new national strategy* (pp. 14-39). New York: Guilford.

Baumrind, D. (1987). A developmental perspective on adolescent risk taking in contemporary America. *New Directions for Child Development, 37*, 93-125.

Beal, C. R. (1994). *Boys and girls: The development of gender roles.* New York: McGraw-Hill.

Beeghly, M., & Cicchetti, D. (1994). Child maltreatment, attachment, and the self system: Emergence of an internal state lexicon in toddlers at high social risk. *Development and Psychopathology, 6*(1), 5-30.

Benard, B., Fafoglia, B., & McDonald, M. (1991). Effective substance abuse prevention: School social workers as catalysts for change. *Social Work in Education, 13*(2), 90-104.

Berrill, K. T. (1990). Anti-gay violence and victimization in the United States: An overview. *Journal of Interpersonal Violence, 5*(3), 274-294.

Bethke, T. M., & DeJoy, D. M. (1993). An experimental study of factors influencing the acceptability of dating violence. *Journal of Interpersonal Violence, 8*(1), 36-51.

Bibby, R. W., & Posterski, D. C. (1992). *Teen trends: A nation in motion.* Toronto: Stoddart.

Biden, J. R. (1993). Violence against women: The congressional response. *American Psychologist, 48*, 1059-1061.

Biringen, Z., Robinson, J. L., & Emde, R. N. (1994). Maternal sensitivity in the second year: Gender-based relations in the dyadic balance of control. *American Journal of Orthopsychiatry, 64*(1), 78-90.

Birns, B., Cascardi, M., & Meyer, S. (1994). Sex-role socialization: Developmental influences on wife abuse. *American Journal of Orthopsychiatry, 64*(1), 50-59.

Blatt, S. J., & Homann, E. (1992). Parent-child interaction in the etiology of dependent and self-critical depression. *Clinical Psychology Review, 12*(1), 47-91.

Blumberg, E. J., Chadwick, M. W., Fogarty, L. A., Speth, T. W., & Chadwick, D. L. (1991). The touch discrimination component of sexual abuse prevention training: Unanticipated positive consequences. *Journal of Interpersonal Violence, 6*(1), 12-28.

Boney-McCoy, S., & Finkelhor, D. (1995). Psychosocial sequelae of violent victimization in a national youth sample. *Journal of Consulting and Clinical Psychology, 63,* 726-736.

Boot camps for young offenders? (1995, July 9). *Toronto Star,* p. F2.

Bowlby, J. (1982). *Attachment and loss: Vol. 1: Attachment* (2nd ed.). New York: Basic Books. (Original work published in 1969)

Bowlby, J. (1972). *Attachment and loss: Vol. 2: Separation, anxiety, and anger.* New York: Basic Books.

Bowlby, J. (1980). *Attachment and loss: Vol. 3: Loss, sadness, and depression.* New York: Basic Books.

Bronfenbrenner, U. (1979). Contexts of child rearing: Problems and prospects. *American Psychologist, 34*(10), 844-850.

Bugental, D. B. (1993). Communication in abusive relationships: Cognitive constructions of interpersonal power. *American Behavioral Scientist, 36,* 288-308.

Burhmester, D., & Furman, W. (1987). The development of companionship and intimacy. *Child Development, 58,* 1101-1113.

Calhoun, J. A. (1992). Youth as resources: A new paradigm in social policy for youth. In G. W. Albee, L. A. Bond, & T. V. C. Monsey (Eds.), *Improving children's lives: Global perspectives on prevention* (pp. 334-341). Newbury Park: Sage.

Came, B., Gillies, L., Howse, J., Kaihla, P., Wickens, B., & Burke, D. (1989, May). Gang terror. *Macleans,* pp. 36-39.

Canadian Press. (1995, September 8). Get tough measures waste time, money. *The London Free Press,* p. A10.

Canadian Radio-Television and Telecommunications Commission (CRTC). (1990). *The portrayal of gender in Canadian broadcasting: 1984-1988* (Content analysis of Canadian broadcasting prepared by George Spears and Kasia Seydegart, Eric Research Inc.). Ottawa: Author.

Carlson, V., Cicchetti, D., Barnett, D., & Brunwald, K. (1989). Disorganized/disoriented attachment relationships in maltreated infants. *Developmental Psychology, 25,* 525-531.

Chavis, D., & Wandersman, A. (1990). Sense of community in the urban environment. A catalyst for participation and community development. *American Journal of Community Psychology, 18*(1), 55-81.

Check, J. V. P., & Malamuth, N. M. (1983). Sex role stereotyping and reactions to depictions of stranger versus acquaintance rape. *Journal of Personality and Social Psychology, 45,* 344-356.

Children's Safety Network. (1991). *A data book of child and adolescent injury.* Washington, DC: National Center for Education in Maternal and Child Health.

Cicchetti, D., & Howes, P. W. (1991). Developmental psychopathology in the context of the family: Illustrations from the study of child maltreatment. *Canadian Journal of Behavioral Science, 23,* 257-281.

Clark, M. L., & Ayers, M. (1993). Friendship expectations and friendship evaluations: Reciprocity and gender effects. *Youth & Society, 24,* 299-313.

Cline, R. W. (1989). The politics of intimacy: Costs and benefits determining disclosure intimacy in male-female dyads. *Journal of Social and Personal Relationships, 6,* 5-20.

Compas, B. E. (1993). Promoting positive mental health during adolescence. In S. G. Millstein, A. C. Petersen, & E. O. Nightingale (Eds.), *Promoting the health of adolescents: New directions for the 21st century* (pp. 159-179). New York: Oxford University Press.

Comstock, G., & Paik, H. (1994). The effects of television violence on antisocial behavior: A meta-analysis. *Communication Research, 21*(4), 516-546.

Covey, S. R. (1989). *The seven habits of highly effective people: Restoring the character ethic.* New York: Simon & Schuster.

Crittenden, P. (1988). Relationships at risk. In J. Belsky & T. Nezworksi (Eds.), *Clinical implications of attachment theory* (pp. 136-174). Hillsdale, NJ: Lawrence Erlbaum.

Crittenden, P., & Ainsworth, M. (1989). Attachment and child abuse. In D. Cicchetti & V. Carlson (Eds.), *Child maltreatment: Theory and research on the causes and consequences of child abuse and neglect* (pp. 432-463). New York: Cambridge University Press.

Crockett, L. J., & Petersen, A. C. (1993). Adolescent development: Health risks and opportunities for health promotion. In S. G. Millstein, A. C. Petersen, & E. O. Nightingale (Eds.), *Promoting the health of adolescents: New directions for the 21st century* (pp. 13-37). New York: Oxford University Press.

Cummings, E. M., Hennessy, K. D., Rabideau, G. J., & Cicchetti, D. (1994). Responses of physically abused boys to interadult anger involving their mothers. *Development and Psychopathology, 6*(1), 31-42.

Davies, P. T., & Cummings, E. M. (1994). Marital conflict and child adjustment: An emotional security hypothesis. *Psychological Bulletin, 116,* 387-411.

Davis, S. M., & Allen, J. P. (1995, April). *Understanding and breaking the cycle of abuse.* Poster session presented at the biennial meeting of the Society for Research in Child Development, Indianapolis, IN.

DeKeseredy, W., & Kelly, K. (1993). The incidence and prevalence of woman abuse in Canadian university and college dating relationships. *Canadian Journal of Sociology, 18,* 137-159.

Deutsch, A. (1949). *The mentally ill in America.* New York: Columbia University Press.

DiCamio, M. (1993). *The encyclopedia of violence: Origins, attitudes, consequences.* New York: Facts on File.

Dix, T. (1991). The affective organization of parenting: Adaptive and maladaptive processes. *Psychological Bulletin, 110*(1), 3-25.

Dobash, R. E., & Dobash, R. P. (1992). *Women, violence, and social change.* New York: Routledge.

Dodge, K. A., Bates, J. E., & Pettit, G. (1990). Mechanisms in the cycle of violence. *Science, 250,* 1678-1683.

Dodge, K. A., Pettit, G. S., & Bates, J. E. (1994). Effects of physical maltreatment on the development of peer relations. *Development and Psychopathology, 6,* 43-55.

Donaldson, S. I., Graham, J. W., & Hansen, W. B. (1994). Testing the generalizability of intervening mechanism theories: Understanding the effects of adolescent drug use and prevention interventions. *Journal of Behavioral Medicine, 17*(2), 195-216.

Doob, A. N., Marinos, V., & Varma, K. (1995). *Youth crime and the youth justice system in Canada: A research perspective.* Toronto: University of Toronto Centre of Criminology.

Dryfoos, J. G. (1991). Adolescents at risk: A summation of work in the field—Programs and policies. *Journal of Adolescent Health, 12,* 630-637.

Duerk, J. (1989). *Circle of stones: Woman's journey to herself.* San Diego: LuraMedia.

Duncan, B. L. (1976). Differential social perception and attribution of intergroup violence: Testing the lower limits of stereotyping of Blacks. *Journal of Personality and Social Psychology, 34,* 590-598.

Dutton, D. G. (1992). Theoretical and empirical perspectives on the etiology and prevention of wife assault. In R. DeV. Peters, R. J. McMahon, & V. L. Quinsey (Eds.), *Aggression and violence throughout the life span* (pp.192-221). Newbury Park, CA: Sage.

Dutton, D. G. (1994). *The domestic assault of women: Psychological and criminal justice perspectives.* Vancouver: University of British Columbia Press.

Dutton, D. G. (1995). Trauma symptoms and PTSD-like profiles in perpetrators of intimate abuse. *Journal of Traumatic Stress, 8,* 299-316.

Dutton, D. G., & Browning, J. J. (1988). Power struggles and intimacy anxieties as causative factors of wife assault. In G. W. Russell (Ed.), *Violence in intimate relationships* (pp. 163-175). New York: PMA Publishing.

Dutton, D. G., & Golant, S. (1995). *The batterer: A psychological profile.* New York: HarperCollins.

Dutton, D. G., & Strachan, C. E. (1987). Motivational needs for power and spouse-specific assertiveness in assaultive and nonassaultive men. *Violence and Victims, 2,* 145-156.

Earls, F., Cairns, R. B., & Mercy, J. A. (1993). The control of violence and the promotion of nonviolence in adolescents. In S. G. Millstein, A. C. Petersen, & E. O. Nightingale (Eds.), *Promoting the health of adolescents: New directions for the 21st century* (pp. 285-304). New York: Oxford University Press.

Eccles, J. S., Midgley, C., Wigfield, A., Buchanan, C. M., Reuman, D., Flanagan, C., & Mac Iver, D. (1993). Development during adolescence: The impact of stage-environment fit on young adolescents' experiences in the schools and in families. *American Psychologist, 48*(2), 90-101.

Elder, G., Caspi, A., & Downey, G. (1986). Problem behavior and family relationships: Life course and intergenerational themes. In A. Sorensen, F. Weinert, & L. Sherrod (Eds.), *Human development: Interdisciplinary perspectives* (pp. 293-340). Hillsdale, NJ: Lawrence Erlbaum.

Elias, R. (1993). *Victims still.* Newbury Park, CA: Sage.

Ellison, C. G., & Powers, D. A. (1994). The contact hypothesis and racial attitudes among Black Americans. *Social Science Quarterly, 75*(2), 385-400.

Else, L., Wonderlich, S. A., Beatty, W. W., Christie, D. W., & Staton, R. D. (1994). Personality characteristics of men who physically abuse women. *Hospital and Community Psychiatry, 44*(1), 54-58.

Emery, K. J. (1993). *Position statement on youth violence prevention and recommended actions.* Dayton, OH: New Futures for Dayton Area Youth, Inc. (ERIC Document Reproduction Service No. ED 357 091)

Erikson, E. H. (1950). *Childhood and society.* New York: Norton.

Eron, L. D. (1982). Parent-child interaction, television violence, and aggression of children. *American Psychologist, 37,* 197-211.

Eron, L. D., Huesmann, L. R., Lefkowitz, M. M., & Walder, L. D. (1972). Does television violence cause aggression? *American Psychologist, 27,* 253-263.

Fagan, J. (1989). The social organization of drug use and drug dealing among urban gangs. *Criminology, 27,* 633-669.

Famularo, R., Kinscherff, R., & Fenton, T. (1992). Parental substance abuse and the nature of child maltreatment. *Child Abuse & Neglect, 16*, 475-483.

Fanshel, D., Finch, S. J., & Grundy, J. F. (1990). *Foster children in life course perspective.* New York: Columbia University Press.

Farber, E. & Egeland, B. (1987). Invulnerability among abused and neglected children. In E. J. Anthony & B. Cohler (Eds.), *The invulnerable child* (pg. 289-314). New York: Guilford.

Feiring, C. (1995). *Lovers as friends: Developing conscious views of romance in adolescence.* Manuscript submitted for publication.

Felmlee, D. H. (1994). Who's on top? Power in romantic relationships. *Sex Roles, 31*, 275-295.

Fisher, J. D., & Fisher, W. A. (1992). Changing AIDS risk behavior. *Psychological Bulletin, 111*, 455-474.

Fiske, S. T., & Taylor, S. E. (1993). *Social cognition* (2nd ed.). New York: McGraw-Hill.

Follette, V. M., & Alexander, P. C. (1992). Dating violence: Current and historical correlates. *Behavioral Assessment, 14*(1), 39-52.

Follingstad, D. R., Wright, S., Lloyd, S., & Sebastian, J. A. (1991). Sex differences in motivations and effects in dating violence. *Family Relations, 40*(1), 51-57.

Fox, J. A., & Pierce, G. (1994, January). American killers are getting younger. *USA Today*, pp. 24-26.

Furman, W., & Buhrmester, D. (1985). Children's perceptions of the personal relationships in their social networks. *Developmental Psychology, 21*, 1014-1024.

Furman, W., & Buhrmester, D. (1992). Age and sex differences in perceptions of networks of personal relationships. *Child Development, 63*(1), 103-115.

Garbarino, J., & Kostelny, K. (1994). Neighborhood-based programs. In G. Melton & F. Barry (Eds.), *Protecting children from abuse and neglect: Foundations for a new national strategy* (pp. 304-352). New York: Guilford.

Gelles, R. J., & Straus, M. A. (1988). *Intimate violence.* New York: Simon & Schuster.

General Accounting Office. (1991, May). *Child abuse prevention: Status of the challenge grant system* (GAO: HRD91-95). Washington, DC: Author.

Gerbner, G., Gross, L., Morgan, M., & Signorielli, N. (1986). Living with television: The dynamics of the cultivation process. In J. Bryant & D. Zillmann (Eds.), *Perspectives on media effects* (pp. 17-41). Hillsdale, NJ: Lawrence Erlbaum.

Gershenson, H. P., Musick, J. S., Ruch-Ross, H. S., Magee, V., Rubino, K. K., & Rosenberg, D. (1989). The prevalence of coercive sexual experience among teenage mothers. *Journal of Interpersonal Violence, 4*, 204-219.

Gibbons, F. X., Helweg-Larsen, M., & Gerrard, M. (1995). Prevalence estimates and adolescent risk behavior: Cross-cultural differences in social influence. *Journal of Applied Psychology, 80*(1), 107-121

Girshick, L. B. (1993). Teen dating violence. *Violence Update, 3*, 1-2, 4, 6.

Gondolf, E. W. (1985). *Men who batter: An integrated approach to stopping wife abuse.* Holmes Beach, FL: Learning Publications.

Greene, M. B. (1993). Chronic exposure to violence and poverty: Interventions that work for youth. *Crime & Delinquency, 39*(1), 106-124.

Gottfredson, M. R., & Hirschi, T. (1995). National crime control policies. *Society, 32*, 30-36.

Greaves, L., Hankivsky, O., & Kingston-Riechers, J. (1995). *Selected estimates of the costs of violence against women.* (Available from the Center for Research on Violence Against Women, 100 Collip Circle, Suite 240, University of Western Ontario Research Park, London, Ontario, N6X 4X8)

Greenberg, M. T., Speltz, M. L., & DeKlyen, M. (1993). The role of attachment in the early development of disruptive behavior problems. *Development and Psychopathology, 5,* 191-213.

Hall, G. C. N., & Hirschman, R. (1991). Toward a theory of sexual aggression: A quadripartite model. *Journal of Consulting and Clinical Psychology, 59,* 662-669.

Hamburg, D. A., Millstein, S. G., Mortimer, A. M., Nightingale, E. O., & Petersen, A. C. (1993). Adolescent health promotion in the 21st century: Current frontiers and future directions. In S. G. Millstein, A. C. Petersen, & E. O. Nightingale (Eds.), *Promoting the health of adolescents: New directions for the 21st century* (pp. 375-388). New York: Oxford University Press.

Harrison, P. A., Hoffmann, N. G., & Edwall, G. E. (1989a). Differential drug use patterns among abused adolescent girls in treatment for chemical dependency. *International Journal of the Addictions, 24,* 499-514.

Harrison, P. A., Hoffmann, N. G., & Edwall, G. E. (1989b). Sexual abuse correlates: Similarities between male and female adolescents in chemical dependency treatment. *Journal of Adolescent Research, 4,* 385-399.

Harter, S. (1990). Self and identity development. In S. S. Feldman & G. R. Elliott (Eds.), *At the threshold: The developing adolescent* (pp. 352-387). Cambridge, MA: Harvard University Press.

Hausman, A. J., Spivak, H., & Prothrow-Stith, D. (1994). Adolescents' knowledge and attitudes about experience with violence. *Journal of Adolescent Health, 15,* 400-406.

Hazan, C., & Shaver, P. (1987). Romantic love conceptualized as an attachment process. *Journal of Personality and Social Psychology, 52,* 511-524.

Hazan, C., & Shaver, P. (1994). Attachment as an organizational framework for research on close relationships. *Psychological Inquiry, 5*(1), 1-22.

Hedin, D., Hannes, K., & Saito, R. (1985). *Minnesota Youth Poll: Youth look at themselves and the world.* Minneapolis: University of Minnesota, Center for Youth Development and Research.

Hedley, M. (1994). The presentation of gendered conflict in popular movies: Affective stereotypes, cultural sentiments, and men's motivation. *Sex Roles, 31,* 721-740.

Hennessy, K. D., Rabideau, G. J., Cicchetti, D., & Cummings, E. M. (1994). Responses of physically abused and nonabused children to different forms of interadult anger. *Child Development, 65,* 815-828.

Herek, G. M. (1993). Documenting prejudice against lesbians and gay men on campus: The Yale sexual orientation survey. *Journal of Homosexuality, 25*(1), 15-30.

Herman, J. L. (1992). *Trauma and recovery: The aftermath of violence—From domestic abuse to political terror.* New York: Basic Books.

Herrenkohl, E. C., Herrenkohl, R. C., & Egolf, B. (1994). Resilient early school-age children from maltreating homes: Outcomes in late adolescence. *American Journal of Orthopsychiatry, 64*(2), 301-309.

Herzberger, S. D., Potts, D. A., & Dillon, M. (1981). Abusive and nonabusive parental treatment from the child's perspective. *Journal of Consulting and Clinical Psychology, 49*(1), 81-90.

Hill, P. (1992). Recent advances in selected aspects of adolescent development. *Journal of Child Psychology and Psychiatry and Allied Disciplines, 34*(1), 69-99.

Holtzworth-Munroe, A. (1992). Social skill deficits in maritally violent men: Interpreting the data using a social information processing model. *Clinical Psychology Review, 12,* 605-617.

Holzworth-Munroe, A., & Anglin, K. (1991). The competency of responses given by maritally violent versus nonviolent men to problematic marital situations. *Violence and Victims, 6,* 257-269.

Hotaling, G. T., & Sugarman, D. B. (1986). An analysis of risk markers in husband to wife violence: The current state of knowledge. *Violence and Victims, 1*(1-2), 101-124.

Huether, J. (1995). Peel public forum keynote presentation. *Journal of the Ontario Association of Children's Aid Societies, 39*(2), 28-31.

Huston A. C., Donnerstein, E., Fairchild, H., Feshback, N. D., Katz, P. A., Murray, J. P., Rubenstein, E. A., Wilcox, B. L., & Zuckerman, D. (1992). *Big world, small screen: The role of television in American society.* Lincoln: University of Nebraska Press.

Jacobson, N. S., Gottman, J. M., Waltz, J., Rushe, R., Babcock, J., & Holtzworth-Munroe, A. (1994). Affect, verbal content, and psychophysiology in the arguments of couples with a violent husband. *Journal of Consulting and Clinical Psychology, 62,* 982-988.

Jessor, R. (1991). Risk behavior in adolescence: A psychosocial framework for understanding and action. *Journal of Adolescent Health, 12,* 597-605.

Jessor, R. (1993). Successful adolescent development among youth in high-risk settings. *American Psychologist, 48*(2), 117-126.

Jussim, L., Nelson, T. E., Manis, M., & Soffin, S. (1995). Prejudice, stereotypes, and labeling effects: Sources of bias in person perception. *Journal of Personality and Social Psychology, 68,* 228-246.

Kahn, M. W., & Fua, C. (1992). Counselor training as a treatment for alcoholism: The helper therapy principle in action. *International Journal of Social Psychiatry, 38,* 208-214.

Kaihla, P. (1995, February 13). Sex offenders: Is there a cure? *Maclean's,* p. 56.

Kalmuss, D. (1984). The intergenerational transmission of marital aggression. *Journal of Marriage and the Family, 46,* 11-19.

Kantrowitz, B., & Wingert, P. (1993, December). A new era of segregation. *Newsweek,* p. 44.

Kaplan, H. B., Johnson, R. J., Bailey, C. A., & Simon, W. (1987). The sociological study of AIDS: A critical review of the literature and suggested research agenda. *Journal of Health and Social Behavior, 28,* 140-157.

Kaufman, J., & Zigler, E. (1987). Do abused children become abusive parents? *American Journal of Orthopsychiatry, 57*(2), 186-192.

Kavanagh, K. A., Youngblade, L., Reid, J. B., & Fagot, B. I. (1988). Interactions between children and abusive versus control parents. *Journal of Clinical Child Psychology, 17*(2), 137-142.

Kazdin, A. E. (1993). Adolescent mental health: Prevention and treatment programs. *American Psychologist, 48,* 127-141.

LaGrange, R. L., & Ferraro, K. F. (1989). Assessing age and gender differences in perceived risk and fear of crime. *Criminology, 27,* 697-719.

Lamb, H. R., & Zusman, J. (1979). Primary prevention in perspective. *American Journal of Psychiatry, 136*(1), 12-17.

Langstaff, D. G. (1991). *Teens as community resources: A model of youth empowerment.* (Available from Plan for Social Excellence, Inc., 116 Radio Circle, Mount Kisco, NY 10549)

Laursen, B., & Collins, W. A. (1994). Interpersonal conflict during adolescence. *Psychological Bulletin, 115,* 197-209.

Lempers, J. D., & Clark-Lempers, D. S. (1992). Young, middle, and late adolescents' comparisons of the functional importance of five significant relationships. *Journal of Youth and Adolescence, 21*(1), 53-96.

Lever, J. (1978). Sex differences in the complexity of children's play and games. *American Sociological Review, 43,* 471-483.

Levine, M. (1981). *The history and politics of community mental health.* New York: Oxford University Press.

Levine, M., & Levine, A. (1970). *A social history of helping services.* New York: Appleton-Century-Crofts.

Levine, M., & Perkins, D. V. (1987). *Principles of community psychology: Perspectives and applications.* New York: Oxford University Press.

Lochman, J. E., Wayland, K. K., & White, K. J. (1993). Social goals: Relationship to adolescent adjustment and to social problem solving. *Journal of Abnormal Child Psychology, 21,* 135-151.

Loeber, R., Weisman, W., & Reid, J. B. (1983). Family interactions of assaultive adolescents, stealers, and nondelinquents. *Journal of Abnormal Child Psychology, 11*(2), 1-14.

Lyons-Ruth, K., Connell, D. B., Grunebaum, H., & Botein, S. (1990). Infants at social risk: Maternal depression and family support services as mediators of infant development and security of attachment. *Child Development, 61*(1), 85-98.

Maheady, L., Sacca, M. K., & Harper, G. F. (1988). Classwide peer tutoring with mildly handicapped high school students. *Exceptional Children, 55*(1), 52-59.

Main, M., & George, C. (1985). Responses of abused and disadvantaged toddlers to distress in agemates: A study in the day care setting. *Developmental Psychology, 21,* 407-412.

Maio, K. (1990, September/October). Hooked on hate? Unfunny comedians, MTV, tabloid television, fright films, and other invasions. *MS. Magazine,* pp. 42-44.

Makepeace, J. M. (1981). Courtship violence among college students. *Family Relations, 30*(1), 97-102.

Malamuth, N., & Briere, J. (1986). Sexual violence in the media: Indirect effects on aggression against women. *Journal of Social Issues, 42*(3), 75-92.

Malamuth, N. M., & Brown, L. M. (1994). Sexually aggressive men's perceptions of women's communications: Testing three explanations. *Journal of Personality and Social Psychology, 67,* 699-712.

Malamuth, N. M., Sockloskie, R. J., Koss, M. P., & Tanaka, J. S. (1991). Characteristics of aggressors against women: Testing a model using a national sample of college students. *Journal of Consulting and Clinical Psychology, 59,* 670-681.

Martin, B. (1990). The transmission of relationship difficulties from one generation to the next. *Journal of Youth and Adolescence, 19,* 181-199.

McCanne, T. R., & Milner, J. S. (1991). Physiological reactivity of physically abusive and at-risk subjects to child-related stimuli. In J. S. Milner (Ed.), *Neuropsychology of aggression* (pp. 147-166). Norwell, MA: Kluwer.

McCord, J. (1990). Comments on "Something that works in juvenile justice." *Evaluation Review, 14,* 612-615.

McWhirter, J. J., McWhirter, B. T., McWhirter, A. M., & McWhirter, E. H. (1993). *At-risk youth: A comprehensive response.* Pacific Grove, CA: Brooks/Cole.

Mesch, D., Lew, M., Johnson, D. W., & Johnson, R. (1986). Isolated teenagers: A psychological self-portrait. New York: Basic Books.

Miedzian, M. (1995). Learning to be violent. In E. Peled, P. G. Jaffe, & J. L. Edleson (Eds.), *Ending the cycle of violence: Community responses to children of battered women* (pp. 10-24). Thousand Oaks, CA: Sage.

Milavsky, J. R., Kessler, R., Stipp, H. H., & Rubens, W. S. (1982). Television and aggression: Results of a panel study. In D. Pearl, L. Bouthilet, & J. Lazar (Eds.), *Television and social behavior: Ten years of scientific progress and implications for the 80s, vol. 2: Technical reviews* (pp. 138-157). Washington, DC: Government Printing Office.

Miller, J. B. (1986). *Toward a new psychology of women.* Boston: Beacon.

Millstein, S. G., & Igra, V. (1995). Theoretical models of adolescent risk-taking behavior. In J. L. Wallander & L. J. Siegel (Eds.), *Adolescent health problems* (pp. 52-71). New York: Guilford.

Millstein, S. G., Petersen, A. C., & Nightingale, E. O. (1993). Adolescent health promotion: Rationale, goals, and objectives. In S. G. Millstein, A. C. Petersen, & E. O. Nightingale (Eds.), *Promoting the health of adolescents: New directions for the 21st century* (pp. 3-10). New York: Oxford University Press.

Milner, J. S. (1993). Social information processing and physical child abuse. *Clinical Psychology Review, 13,* 275-294.

Milner, J. S., & Chilamkurti, C. (1991). Physical child abuse perpetrator characteristics: A review of the literature. *Journal of Interpersonal Violence, 6,* 345-366.

Morganthau, T., Mabry, M., Genao, L., & Washington, F. (1991, May 6). Race on campus: Failing the test? *Newsweek,* pp. 26-27.

Morganthau, T., Springen, K., Smith, V. E., Rosenberg, D., Beale, G., Bogert, C., Gegax, T. T., & Joseph, N. (1994, December 12). The orphanage. *Newsweek,* pp. 28-32.

Morrill, W. A. (1993). Seeking better outcomes for children and families. *National Center for Service Integration News, 1,* 1-2.

Mueller, E., & Silverman, N. (1989). Peer relations in maltreated children. In D. Cicchetti & V. Carlson (Eds.), *Child maltreatment: Theory and research on the causes and consequences of child abuse and neglect* (pp. 529-578). Cambridge: Cambridge University Press.

Murphy, C. M., Meyer, S., & O'Leary, K. D. (1994). Dependency characteristics of partner assaultive men. *Journal of Abnormal Psychology, 103,* 729-735.

Murray, B. (1995, September). Kids learn keys to healthy relationships. *APA Monitor, 26,* p. 48.

Murray, J. P. (1995). Children and television violence. *Kansas Journal of Law and Public Policy, 4,* 7-14.

National Association for the Education of Young Children (1990). NAEYC position statement on media violence in children's lives. *Young Children, 45,* 18-21.

National Research Council. (1993a). *Losing generations: Adolescents in high-risk settings.* Washington, DC: National Academy Press.

National Research Council. (1993b). *Understanding child abuse and neglect* (Panel on Research on Child Abuse and Neglect). Washington, DC: National Academy Press.

Offer, D., & Ostrov, E. (1981). *The adolescent: A psychological self-portrait.* New York: Basic Books.

Oldershaw, L., Walters, G. C., & Hall, D. K. (1986). Control strategies and noncompliance in abusive mother-child dyads: An observational study. *Child Development, 57,* 722-732.

Olds, D. (in press). Child abuse prevention. In D. A. Wolfe, R. McMahon, & R. Dev. Peters (Eds.), *Child abuse: New directions in prevention and treatment across the lifespan.* Thousand Oaks, CA: Sage.

Olds, D., Henderson, C. R., Phelps, C., Kitman, H., Hanks, C. (1993). Effect of prenatal and infancy nurse home visitation on government spending. *Medical Care, 31,*(2) 155-174.

O'Leary, K. D., Malone, J., & Tyree, A. (1994). Physical aggression in early marriage: Prerelationship and relationship effects. *Journal of Consulting and Clinical Psychology, 62,* 594-602.

Oliver, J. E. (1993). Intergenerational transmission of child abuse: Rates, research, and clinical implications. *American Journal of Psychiatry, 150*(9), 1315-1324.

Patterson, G. R., DeBaryshe, B. D., & Ramsey, E. (1989). A developmental perspective on antisocial behavior. *American Psychologist, 44,* 329-335.

Paulson, M. J., Coombs, R. H., & Landsverk, J. (1990). Youth who physically assault their parents. *Journal of Family Violence, 5*(2), 121-133.

Pence, E., & Paymar, M. (1993). *Education groups for men who batter: The Deluth model.* New York: Springer.

Peterson, D. L., & Pfost, K. S. (1989). Influence of rock videos on attitudes of violence against women. *Psychological Reports, 64,* 319-322.

Pinderhughes, H. (1993). The anatomy of racially motivated violence in New York city: A case study of youth in southern Brooklyn. *Social Problems, 40*(4), 478-492.

Pleck, J. H., Sonenstein, F. L., & Ku, L. (1993). Masculinity ideology: Its impact on adolescent males' relationships. *Journal of Social Issues, 49*(3), 11-19.

Pollitt, K. (1991, April 7). The Smurfette principle. *New York Times Magazine,* pp. 22-24.

Prison spending outpaces social services. (1993, October 3). *Toronto Star,* p. B5.

Prochaska, J., DiClemente, C., & Norcross, J. (1992). In search of how people change. *American Psychologist, 47,* 1102-1114.

Pryor, D. W., & McGarrell, E. F. (1993). Public perceptions of youth gang crime: An exploratory analysis. *Youth & Society, 24,* 399-418.

Quadrel, M. J., Fischhoff, B., & Davis, W. (1993). Adolescent (in)vulnerability. *American Psychologist, 48*(2), 102-116.

Reider, C., & Cicchetti, D. (1989). Organizational perspective on cognitive control functioning and cognitive-affective balance in maltreated children. *Developmental Psychology, 25,* 382-393.

Reissman, F. (1965). The "helper-therapy" principle. *Social Work, 10,* 24-32.

Reno, J. (1994, January). How to save our children. *USA Today,* pp. 36-39.

Riley, R. E. (1994, January). Curbing youth violence. *USA Today,* pp. 36-39.

Rogers, K. (1994). Wife assault: The findings of a national survey. *Juristat, 14*(9), 1-22.

Rooney-Rebeck, P., & Jason, L. (1986). Prevention of prejudice in elementary school students. *Journal of Primary Prevention, 7*(2), 63-73.

Roscoe, B. (1985). Courtship violence: Acceptable forms and situations. *College Student Journal, 19*, 389-393.

Roth, J. (1994). Understanding and preventing violence. *National Institute of Justice: Research in Brief.* Washington, DC: U.S. Department of Justice. Quoted from the Internet.

Rubin, K. H., & Krasnor, L. R. (1986). Social-cognitive and social-behavioral perspective on problem-solving. In M. Perlmutter (Ed.), *The Minnesota Symposium of Child Psychology: Vol. 18. Cognitive perspectives on children's social and behavioral development* (pp. 1-68). Hillsdale, NJ: Lawrence Erlbaum.

Rutter, M. (1987). Psychosocial resilience and protective mechanisms. *American Journal of Orthopsychiatry, 57*, 316-333.

Ryan, C., Mathews, F., & Banner, J. (1993). *Student perceptions of violence: Executive summary of preliminary findings.* (Available from Central Toronto Youth Services, 65 Wellesley St. E., Suite 300, Toronto, ON, M4Y, 1G7)

Rzepnicki, T., & Stein, T. J. (1985). Permanency planning for children in foster care: A review of projects. *Children and Youth Services Review, 7*(2-3), 92-108.

Salzinger, S., Feldman, R. S., Hammer, M., & Rosario, M. (1993). The effects of physical abuse on children's social relationships. *Child Development, 64*, 169-187.

Sanderson, C. A., & Cantor, N. (1995). Social dating goals in late adolescence: Implications for safer sexual activity. *Journal of Personality and Social Psychology, 68*, 1121-1134.

Saunders, D. G. (1992). A typology of men who batter: Three types derived from cluster analysis. *American Journal of Orthopsychiatry, 62*(2), 264-275.

Schaefer, C. (1978). *How to influence children.* New York: Van Nostrand Reinhold.

Schechter, S., & Edleson, J. L. (1994). "In the best interest of women and children: A call for collaboration between child welfare and domestic violence constituencies." (Brief prepared for a conference sponsored by the University of Iowa School of Social Work and the Johnson Foundation on *Violence and Child Welfare: Integrating Policy and Practice for Families,* Racine, WI.)

Serbin, L. A., Powlishta, K. K., & Gulko, J. (1993). The development of sex typing in middle childhood. *Monographs of the Society for Research in Child Development, 58*(Serial No. 232).

Shapiro, J. P., Baumeister, R. F., & Kessler, J. W. (1991). A three-component model of children's teasing: Aggression, humor, and ambiguity. *Journal of Social and Clinical Psychology, 10*, 459-472.

Shealy, C. N. (1995). From Boys Town to Oliver Twist: Separating fact from fiction in welfare reform and out-of-home placement of children and youth. *American Psychologist, 50*, 565-580.

Shields, A. M., Cicchetti, D., & Ryan, R. M. (1994). The development of emotional and behavioral self-regulation and social competence among maltreated school-aged children. *Development and Psychopathology, 6*(1), 57-75.

Shyne, A., & Schroeder, A. (1978). *National Study of Social Services to Children and Their Families—Overview.* Washington, DC: Children's Bureau, U.S. Department of Health and Human Services.

Signorielli, N. (1991). *A sourcebook on children and television.* New York: Greenwood.

Sisson, L. A., Van-Hasselt, V. B., Hersen, M., & Strain, M. (1985). Peer interventions: Increasing social behaviors in multihandicapped children. *Behavior Modification, 9*(3), 293-321.

Slavin, R., & Oickle, E. (1981). Effects of cooperative learning teams on student achievement and race relations: Treatment by race interactions. *Sociology of Education, 54,* 174-180.

Sluckin, A. (1981). *Growing up on the playground.* Boston: Routledge & Kegan Paul.

Spergel, I. A. (1992). Youth gangs: An essay review. *Social Services Review, 66*(1), 122-140.

Sroufe, L. A. (1989). Relationships, self and individual adaptation. In A. J. Sameroff & R. N. Emde (Eds.), *Relationship disturbances on early childhood: A developmental approach* (pp. 70-94). New York: Basic Books.

Sroufe, L. A., & Fleeson, J. (1986). Attachment and the construction of relationships. In W. W. Hartup & Z. Rubin (Eds.), *Relationships and development* (pp. 51-71). Hillsdale, NJ: Lawrence Erlbaum.

Statistics Canada. (1993). *Violence Against Women Survey.* Ottawa, ON: Author.

Stith, S. M., & Farley, S. C. (1993). A predictive model of male spousal violence. *Journal of Family Violence, 8,* 183-201.

Strassberg, Z., & Dodge, K. A. (1995). *Maternal physical abuse of the child: A social information processing perspective.* Unpublished manuscript, Vanderbilt University.

Straus, M. A., & Kantor, G. K. (1994). Corporal punishment of adolescents by parents: A risk factor in the epidemiology of depression, suicide, alcohol abuse, child abuse, and wife beating. *Adolescence, 29,* 543-561.

Strouse, J. S., Buerkel-Rothfuss, N., & Long, E. C. J. (1995). Gender and family as moderators of the relationship between music video exposure and adolescent sexual permissiveness. *Adolescence, 30,* 505-521.

Sudermann, M., & Jaffe, P. (1993, August). *Dating violence among a sample of 1,567 high school students.* Paper presented at the annual meeting of the American Psychological Association, Toronto.

Sudermann, M., Jaffe, P. G., & Hastings, E. (1995). Violence prevention programs in secondary (high) schools. In E. Peled, P. G. Jaffe, & J. L. Edleson (Eds.), *Ending the cycle of violence: Community responses to children of battered women* (pp. 232-254). Thousand Oaks, CA: Sage.

Surrey, J. L. (1991). The "self-in-relation": A theory of women's development. In J. D. Jordan, A. G. Kaplan, J. B. Miller, I. P. Stiver, & J. L. Surrey (Eds.), *Women's growth in connection* (pp. 162-180). New York: Guilford.

Swim, J. K., Aikin, K. J., Hall, W. S., & Hunter, B. A. (1995). Sexism and racism: Old-fashioned and modern prejudices. *Journal of Personality and Social Psychology, 68,* 199-214.

Takanishi, R. (1993). The opportunities for adolescence—Research, interventions, and policy. *American Psychologist, 48*(2), 85-87.

Tannen, D. (1991). *That's not what I meant!* New York: Simon & Schuster.

Tate, D. C., Reppucci, N. D., & Mulvey, E. P. (1995). Violent juvenile delinquents: Treatment effectiveness and implications for future action. *American Psychologist, 50,* 777-781.

Thompson, R. A. (1995). *Preventing child maltreatment through social support: A critical analysis.* Thousand Oaks, CA: Sage.

Thompson, R. A., & Wilcox, B. L. (1995). Child maltreatment research: Federal support and policy issues. *American Psychologist, 50,* 789-793.

Trickett, P. K., & Susman, E. J. (1988). Parental perceptions of child-rearing practices in physically abusive and nonabusive families. *Developmental Psychology, 22,* 115-123.

U.S. Advisory Board on Child Abuse and Neglect. (1990). *Child abuse and neglect: Critical first steps in response to a national emergency* (Stock No. 017-092-00104-5). Washington, DC: Government Printing Office.

U.S. Advisory Board on Child Abuse and Neglect. (1991). *Creating caring communities: Blueprint for an effective federal policy on child abuse and neglect.* Washington, DC: Author.

U.S. Advisory Board on Child Abuse and Neglect. (1995). *A nation's shame: Fatal child abuse and neglect in the United States* (Department of Health and Human Services Administration for Children and Families: Fifth Report). Washington, DC: Department of Health and Human Services.

U.S. Senate Judiciary Committee. (1992, October). *Violence against women: A week in the life of America* (Prepared by the majority staff of the Senate Judiciary Committee). (Available from Hart Office Building, Room B04, Washington, DC 20510)

Van Biema, D. (1995, December 11). Abandoned to her fate. *Time,* pp. 38-42.

Van de Van, P. (1995). Talking with juvenile offenders about gay males and lesbians: Implications for combating homophobia. *Adolescence, 30*(117), 19-42.

Violence in the schools mimics big city violence. (1993, November 3). *The Daily News,* p. A6.

Vuchinich, S., Bank, L., & Patterson, G. R. (1992). Parenting, peers, and the stability of antisocial behavior in preadolescent boys. *Developmental Psychology, 28,* 510-521.

Wahler, R. G., & Dumas, J. E. (1986). Maintenance factors in coercive mother-child interactions: The compliance and predictability hypotheses. *Journal of Applied Behavior Analysis, 19*(1), 13-22.

Walker, L. E. A. (1979). *The battered woman.* New York: Harper and Row.

Walker, L. E. A. (1989). Psychology and violence against women. *American Psychologist, 44,* 695-702.

Wallerstein, N. (1992). Powerlessness, empowerment, and health: Implications for health promotion programs. *American Journal of Health Promotion, 6*(3), 197-205.

Waters, E., Posada, G., Crowell, J., & Lay, K. (1993). Is attachment theory ready to contribute to our understanding of disruptive behavior problems? *Development and Psychopathology, 5,* 215-224.

Wekerle, C., & Wolfe, D. A. (1996). Child maltreatment. In E. J. Mash & R. Barclay (Eds.), *Child psychopathology* (pp. 492-537). New York: Guilford.

Wekerle, C., Wolfe, D. A., & Lefebvre, L. (1995). *History of child maltreatment and adolescent insecure attachment models: The double relationship whammy.* Manuscript submitted for publication.

Whaley, A. L. (1992). A culturally sensitive approach to the prevention of interpersonal violence among urban Black youth. *Journal of the National Medical Association, 84,* 585-588.

Whitaker, M., Starr, M., McCormick, J., Smith, V. E., Mabry, M., Wright, L., & Carroll, G. (1991, May 6). A crisis of shattered dreams. *Newsweek,* pp. 28-31.

Widom, C. S. (1989). Does violence beget violence? A critical examination of the literature. *Psychological Bulletin, 106*(1) 3-28.

Wilson, M., & Daly, M. (1994). Spousal homicide. *Juristat, 14*(8), 1-15.

Wilson-Brewer, R. (1991, July). *Violence prevention for young adolescents: A survey of the state of the art* (Working papers). Paper presented at the Carnegie Corporation Conference on Violence Prevention for Young Adolescents, Education Development Center, Cambridge, MA.

Wolfe, D. A. (1991). *Preventing physical and emotional abuse of children.* New York: Guilford.

Wolfe, D. A., & Jaffe, P. (1991). Child abuse and family violence as determinants of child psychopathology. *Canadian Journal of Behavioural Science, 23,* 282-299.

Wolfe, D. A., & McGee, R. (1994). Dimensions of child maltreatment and their relationship to adolescent adjustment. *Development and Psychopathology, 6,* 165-181.

Wolfe, D. A., Reppucci, N. D., & Hart, S. (1995). Child abuse prevention: Knowledge and priorities. *Journal of Clinical Child Psychology, 24*(1), 5-22.

Wolfe, D. A., Wekerle, C., Reitzel-Jaffe, D., & Gough, R. (1995). Promoting healthy, nonviolent relationships among at-risk youth. In E. Peled, P. Jaffe, & J. Edelson (Eds.), *Ending the cycle of violence: Community responses to children of battered women* (pp. 255-274). Thousand Oaks, CA: Sage.

Wolfe, D. A., Wekerle, C., Reitzel-Jaffe, D., & Lefebvre, L. (1995). *Factors associated with increased risk of gender-based violence among adolescents.* Manuscript submitted for publication.

Wolfe, D. A., Wekerle, C., Gough, R., Reitzel-Jaffe, D., Grasley, C., Pittman, A. L., Lefebvre, L., & Stumpf, J. (1996). *The youth relationships manual: A group approach with adolescents for the prevention of woman abuse and the promotion of healthy relationships.* Thousand Oaks, CA: Sage.

Yakabuski, K. (1994, April 17). Nipping crime in the bud. *The Toronto Star,* C1, C4.

Young, G. (1994). Trends in justice spending—1988/1989 to 1992/1993. *Juristat, 14*(16), 1-15.

Zimmerman, M. A., & Rappaport, J. (1988). Citizen participation, perceived control, and psychological empowerment. *American Journal of Community Psychology, 16*(5), 725-750.

Zinsmeister, K. (1990, June). Growing up scared: Spurred on by family instability, violent crime now touches millions of young lives. *Atlantic,* pp. 49-52.

Index

About the Authors

David A. Wolfe is Professor of Psychology and Psychiatry at the University of Western Ontario in London, Canada, and a founding member of the Center for Research on Violence Against Women and Children in London. His interests in youth empowerment as a means to prevent personal violence derive from 20 years of research on child abuse and neglect and his resultant view that these phenomena are preventable. He is author of numerous articles and books on the broad topic of child abuse and domestic violence, including *Children of Battered Women* (with P. Jaffe and S. Wilson; Sage, 1990); *Child Abuse: Implications for Child Development and Psychopathology* (Sage, 1987); *Preventing Physical and Emotional Abuse of Children* (Guilford, 1991), and the companion manual to this book, *The Youth Relationships Manual* (Sage, 1996).

Christine Wekerle is Assistant Professor of Psychology at York University, where she enjoys teaching in the area of developmental psychopathology and child clinical psychology. Her interests in child abuse research have grown in parallel with her other work related to children and families, including parenting problems and

181

child maladjustment. She has published articles and chapters pertaining to the link between child maltreatment and adolescent outcomes, and she is coauthor of *The Youth Relationships Manual* (Sage, 1996).

Katreena Scott is currently completing her Ph.D. in clinical child psychology at the University of Western Ontario. She was worked previously with the research team for the Better Beginnings, Better Futures Project in Ontario, a community-based project to prevent childhood disorders. Her research interests center on the promotion of healthy functioning among children and adolescents, and on the broad implementation of prevention initiatives.